Monitoring and Evaluation in the early years

Assessing the effectiveness of what we do

by Pennie Akehurst

Contents

Published by Practical Pre-School Books, A Division of MA Education Ltd, St Jude's Church, Dulwich Road, Herne Hill, London, SE24 0PB.
Tel: 020 7738 5454 www.practicalpreschoolbooks.com © MA Education Ltd 2019. All photos © MA Education Ltd.
Design: Mary Holmes **fonthill**creative 01722 717036

ISBN 978-1-912611-05-8

Introduction

Since the introduction of 'The Curriculum Guidance for the Foundation Stage' in 2000, there have been incremental changes to the way in which the early years private, voluntary and independent sector has been inspected.

These changes have moved practice away from the need to evidence that something is in place to demonstrating its effectiveness. Leaders and managers are now expected to have a clear view of the quality of their provision and to be able to show that they understand what is working well, what isn't, and that they take swift and effective action to address any issues that they find. This means that leaders and managers now need to have a far greater breadth of knowledge than ever before.

Continuing to develop our knowledge and understanding as leaders and managers is of critical importance for many reasons (some of which I'll touch on later), but the most concerning of those reasons is because our inspection outcome is directly linked to the funding that we receive from our local authority.

Receiving an inadequate inspection outcome under the Department for Education's current Early Education and Childcare, Statutory Guidance for Local Authorities means that local authorities have a statutory duty to remove early education funding as soon as an *inadequate* inspection outcome is published (DfE, 2018). The statutory guidance also makes provision for local authorities to remove 2-year-old funding if a setting receives a judgement of *requires improvement*. There is, therefore, a real imperative for leaders and managers to continue to develop their understanding of pedagogy, practice, business and leadership if provision is to survive.

This book has been written to support the work of education management professionals in the private, voluntary and independent sector. It is for our leaders and managers of today, those of the future and anyone working in a support or quality assurance role.

To current leaders and managers. This guide aims to broaden your understanding of governance and business strategy with the intention of helping you to enhance your current monitoring and evaluation systems. I have provided you with a roadmap for a systematic approach to the development of business strategy because without these foundations, we cannot guarantee that we are monitoring and evaluating the things that are of greatest importance to our setting and our future sustainability.

To those studying early years or considering a post in management. It is important for students and practitioners to understand what good monitoring and evaluation looks like so that you can contribute to the design of systems and processes that help everyone to understand what is working well and where there is room for improvement. It is also important to have this level of knowledge so that you can challenge poor leadership and management in a way that encourages growth.

I also hope that the content of this book will support you well when you finally move into a leadership position, as knowing how to 'set out your stall' is half the battle!

To anyone working in an advisory capacity (advisory teachers, consultants, area managers, those working in a quality assurance role and lecturers). Our role is crucial in supporting leaders and managers to understand that:

- Quick fixes will only ever be short-lived and that they do not bring about sustainable improvement.
- Practice isn't necessarily in a good place just because a team can satisfactorily answer all the questions that they can think of.
- A good (or better) inspection outcome does not mean that they can stop horizon scanning for things that may affect their business or practice in the future.

Leaders and managers often don't know, what they don't know, so staff teams need to constantly and consistently be outward-looking to bring knowledge and information back into their settings. Our role is to support leaders, managers and practitioners to become resilient in a climate of constant change, and to inspire them to want to know more so that they can make informed decisions about practice, respond positively to change and bring about success.

Why a book on monitoring and self-evaluation?

Quite simply, because it is long overdue. I have worked in early years for the best part of three decades as a practitioner, leader and manager, in quality improvement advisory roles and then as a leader of early years and childcare services in two local authorities; in all that time I have never come across one document that adequately

and succinctly explains business strategy and the important role it plays in establishing effective monitoring and evaluation systems, from the point of view of a pre-school, playgroup or nursery chain.

The need for this book became even more apparent when I decided to leave my role in my local authority to establish Early Years Fundamentals; a company that focuses on understanding and explaining why large numbers of settings (nationally) fall into 'inadequate' or 'requires improvement' categories.

I came to realise that there just isn't enough information out there for leaders and managers on the nuts and bolts of how to put effective monitoring systems in place and then how to use that information to respond to change and to drive sustainable improvements. My research has led me to believe that business strategy is absent in many settings, which means that leaders and managers may not have a clear rationale for what they do and how they do it. That, in turn, causes worry about whether they are monitoring the right things and if they have gone into enough depth as, in some cases, gaps in practice could be overlooked.

This book is not about quick fixes. It is a systematic approach to developing robust and effective monitoring and self-evaluation systems which has to start with the development of a business strategy. The approaches advocated in this book will, therefore, take time, perseverance and commitment.

It is worth remembering that monitoring and evaluation is a complex discipline which extends beyond what we do with children, therefore, it will take time to understand. Keep in mind that if the pursuit of excellence was easy, every setting would be outstanding!

Chapter 1: The basis of effective monitoring systems and processes

This book aims to provide the roadmap for any setting to become really great at what they do. I have chosen not to use Ofsted's terminology of 'Outstanding' because that tends to focus the mind on what is written in the Early Years Inspection Handbook, whereas I want to give you the time and space to focus on good business strategy and effective management practices that will ensure that what you do, day in, day out, is of a consistently high standard. With those systems in place, outstanding judgements will come and, more importantly, will be sustained.

Business strategy hasn't really featured on the radar of many leaders, managers and quality improvement consultants because early years courses and qualifications have heavily focused on pedagogy and practice. This is as it should be because tuning into children to meet their individual needs and supporting them to flourish is our core business.

It requires a high level of skill and an in-depth knowledge of child development and how children learn, but when we move into a management role, there is also a need for us to have a wider view of what we do and how we do it. We need to be able to look beyond pedagogy and practice. This resource has been designed so that you can follow a process that will enable you and your team to reflect on what is currently in place and to identify changes that will increase the effectiveness of what you do, and the quality of what children receive.

Why we need a business strategy

We need a business strategy because it is the only way to ensure that we are clear about our setting's purpose and that what we do at every level of our provision contributes to that purpose.

There is a huge amount of research about the development of effective monitoring systems both in education and out in the wider world of industry, but that isn't a helpful place for us to start as the vast majority of that work assumes that we already know what needs to be in place before we can start to focus on what is working well and what isn't. So, to ensure that we have a solid foundation for our monitoring and evaluation activities, we are going back to basics to make sure that we haven't left anything fundamental out.

In this first chapter, we are going to spend time unpicking how to put a business strategy together; our journey, therefore, needs to start with our purpose or, as motivational speaker and organisation consultant Simon Sinek puts it, 'our WHY'.

In his numerous YouTube video clips, books and interviews, Simon has been able to identify the root cause of so many of the problems that we face in our daily work as leaders and managers. He describes it as losing our WHY or core purpose.

Simon's research would lead him to believe that staff in a huge number of organisations know what they do, and how they do it, but very few of those staff members will know specifically why they do it. When he talks about the WHY, he's not talking about what motivates individuals in particular, for example, being able to pay the bills or to pay the mortgage. He's talking about our setting's WHY, which is the reason our pre-school or nursery exists…our purpose or our ultimate goal.
(Sinek, S. 2009.)

Finding your WHY

In early years, a setting's purpose is often developed around the themes of providing children with solid foundations for later learning, helping children to fulfil their potential and the need to keep our youngest and, in some cases, most vulnerable children safe.

These types of phrases can often be found in the publicity materials that we provide for parents, but it is rare to find a setting that has invested time in constructing what they do around these statements, and, more often than not, most of the settings and the staff that I work with will have some differing views as to why their setting exists.

As I go around the room, staff members will make an educated guess as to what their setting's core purpose is or will share their own thoughts on why the setting exists, however, very few of them will be able to share their WHY with accuracy.

Our WHY is a critical part of our business strategy; it gives staff a greater insight into their role and enables them to connect what they do on a daily basis with the overall goals of our setting. It, therefore, isn't enough for staff to think that they know our setting's WHY. They need to know AND internalise it. That connection must not be underestimated as it creates a shared sense of purpose and responsibility that ties us all together, and that is the very basis of teamwork.

What might your WHY look like?

Our purpose should be meaningful. It needs to mean something to our staff, to those who use our services and to our children. However, it isn't always easy to communicate it. How can we explain what we're here to do and what is important to us?

If you feel that your WHY is missing and are unsure of where to start, there are some examples of WHYs below. At the very least you will be able to use these statements to open a conversation about what you do and don't like and what you believe is right for your setting with your team.

- To provide children with high quality environments and highly-skilled staff that can support them to explore and learn about the world around them.
- To create meaningful relationships with families ensuring that we work together to meet the individual needs of their child so that they may flourish.
- To provide children with inspiring learning environments and highly-skilled staff who can help each child to develop their unique skills and talents.
- To provide a learning community in which children and adults learn together, and where children can explore and investigate the world around them in a safe environment that enables them to develop their knowledge, skills, confidence and resilience.

The most important thing is that our WHY clearly communicates the reasons for our existence and that it then drives what we do.

Task 1. - Your WHY

Do you have a WHY? If not, why does your setting exist? What is it there to do?
If you have a WHY, does it still fit and make sense, or does it need to change?
If it needs to change, who should be involved to ensure that your WHY has meaning for staff, parents and children?

When highly effective leadership teams start with their setting's WHY, it becomes far easier to develop a framework that enables them to think about how they are going to get there and what that **should** look like in practice. This framework is important because our monitoring and evaluation systems will flow from the WHY, HOW and WHAT we do.

First, we need to be clear that vision, mission statements and values are not the same as our WHY. If we do not define our WHY first, we'll not know whether our vision is taking us in the right direction, our mission statement is right for our setting or if our values uphold our purpose.

Our WHY should also be shaped by our pedagogy or the how and what we believe children should learn or have experience of during their time with us.

Our WHY will be much stronger if staff members have been involved in its development. It creates a sense of ownership and deepens each person's understanding of it and its importance. If staff members are not able to be part of the creation of the WHY, dedicated time will need to be spent developing a shared understanding across our staff team.

THINK ABOUT...

If you believe that your WHY is firmly in place, how do you know that staff have internalised it? Just having it in your staff handbook or in induction materials will not help staff to connect their roles and responsibilites with your setting's purpose. It needs some dedicated talk time so that you can make sure that everyone is on the same page.

Task 2. - Do staff know your WHY?

Check out the understanding of your staff team. Ask them 'Why does our setting exist? What are we here to do?'

It is best not to do this activity as a group as you want to understand each member of staff's understanding. Ask everyone to take those two questions away and to think about their answers, then collect everyone's thoughts and compare them with your own.

Are you all on the same page? Does everyone even understand the question, or have they given you their own personal WHY? You may find that you need to spend time discussing what your WHY/purpose means with your staff team.

Until we all have the same level of understanding, our WHY will just be words on a piece of paper. It is worth remembering that a team cannot truly be effective if they do not understand their purpose.

Making your WHY happen

With our WHY firmly established, the next logical question is HOW are we going to make this happen?

This is a critical step in developing our business strategy as it helps us to identify important areas of work that contribute overall to the running of a successful early years setting.

Using one of the WHYs from the earlier examples, we can unpick this process in more detail.

Why do we exist? (WHY)

Our purpose is to provide children with high quality environments and highly skilled staff that can support them to explore and learn about the world around them.

To understand our HOW, we need to analyse or take apart our WHY. We need to ask ourselves what key areas of work will help us to make our WHY a reality.

Let's just take the first part of our WHY and start to understand the key areas of work needed to successfully implement this part of the statement.

"Our purpose is to provide children with high quality environments… "

Below are the types of responses that we could expect from our team.

How are we going to make this happen? (HOW)
We need to understand what research is telling us about effective learning environments for the different age groups of children that we support.
We need to adopt a rationale for our environments based on what we want children to learn and experience (our pedagogy).
We need to provide well-resourced environments both inside and outside which enable us to deliver a broad and balanced curriculum.
We need to provide environments that are safe for children to explore and investigate.
We need to identify the on-going needs of the communities that we serve so that our activities, experiences and environments provide appropriate support and opportunities.
We need to provide environments that motivate children to investigate, explore and question.
We need to provide environments where children can lead their own learning by making choices about where they want to learn in the environment, what they need to use and who they need to help them.

This is not an exhaustive list, but by putting some thought into how we are going to make our WHY happen, we will start to generate a list of statements that will reflect our knowledge of pedagogy and the principles that underpin effective early years practice.

Again, going through this process with our team will help to create a deeper level of understanding and ownership, but it also brings other benefits. Having several people sitting around the table means that we have a greater range of knowledge and experience to draw on. The more

of our team members we involve, the less likely we are to miss out something important (although you may just want to involve senior leaders in larger settings as too many people can be counterproductive!)

Being realistic, there are going to be many leadership teams who simply cannot afford to pull all staff members together to go through this process. In this situation, the leadership team will need to find ways of including staff members in the development of the WHY and HOW. Maybe you could put together an initial draft and then take it to your team for consultation or use some initial thoughts as a development item during a team meeting.

The 'how we're going to make it happen' isn't just about the things that we need to do and provide for our children. There are also a number of hidden elements that contribute to achieving our purpose and the smooth running of our setting. We will, therefore, be required to consider the need for or implications of:

- legislation and local guidance on the safeguarding,
- employment law and safer recruitment practices,
- data handling (GDPR),
- Health & Safety legislation,
- financial law,
- financial planning,
- marketing.

There are likely to be other things that we will add to this list, but the examples above provide a good starting point.

The reality is that if we do not include these elements, our business will limp along at best or could close due to sustainability issues, breaches in legislation or because not enough people know about what we do and where to find us.

Business strategy is much more than developing our purpose and unpicking its meaning. We need to pay just as much attention to complying with legislative requirements, financial planning, employment law and marketing etc, if we want our setting to remain viable for future generations!

When you are unpicking your HOW, you will need to use the EYFS statutory framework to identify important areas of work.

This is not about identifying individual statutory requirements but using the general headings in the EYFS such as Staff:child ratios, Key person and Health to create important strands of our work. For example, we need to ensure that staff are suitable to work with children, and that we adhere to the requirements for qualifications and ratios.

You will need to unpick each of these key areas/pieces of legislation or statutory guidance in exactly the same way as we did for our purpose. This is to make sure that nothing important is missed.

Your WHAT (defining your outcomes for success)

We know why we exist, and we have identified how we are going to make it happen, so, our focus now needs to move onto our WHAT.

In this streamlined process, our WHAT is what we would expect to see if we were successful. To do this, we need to take each of our HOWs and break them down further so that we have something tangible to work to. Think of them as outcomes for success.

To help us do this we may want to use questions like the ones below:

- What would need to be in place?
- What would be happening?
- What would staff be doing?
- What would the environment look like?

Here is an example which uses 3 of the statements from our HOW list. There are likely to be other things that could be added to our list of WHATs, but the example demonstrates how influential our WHY, HOW and WHAT are for practice.

Task 3. – How are you going to make your WHY happen?

Spend some time thinking about all the key areas of work that will ensure that your WHY or purpose happens. What is it going to take to run a successful setting?

If you are doing this with your team or senior leaders, ask them to write down their thoughts individually first as this is likely to produce a greater range of areas to discuss.

To make sure that you have time to discuss the entirety of your WHY statement and those important hidden elements, you may need to limit the amount of time that you spend on each part. If you don't you could end up discussing just one aspect of your purpose all meeting.

Keep a copy of documents like the EYFS, Working Together etc. handy so that you can make sure that all the important parts of legislation are covered.

IMPORTANT: You are not identifying actions, but key areas of work that will make your setting run smoothly. At this point we're just starting to create the framework for our business, the detail comes later!

Our purpose	
To provide children with high quality environments and highly skilled staff that can support them to explore and learn about the world around them.	
How?	**What?**
We need to provide well-resourced environments both inside and outside which enable us to deliver a broad and balanced curriculum.	■ The 7 areas of learning will be well represented in our resources and equipment. ■ There will be a range of open-ended resources across our environments. ■ Our enviornments and resources will be representative of the communities we serve. ■ Our resources will ensure that children have a wider world view. ■ Areas of learning will be evident in our indoor environment. ■ Areas of learning will be evident in our outdoor environment
We need to provide environments that are safe for children to explore and investigate.	■ The indoor environment will be secure. ■ The outdoor environment will be secure. ■ All adults will be suitable to work with children. ■ Toys and equipment will be in a good state of repair and appropriate for the age group with which we work. ■ Staff will be able to identify and remove or reduce potential hazards. ■ Staff will be able to identify and manage risk.
We need to provide environments where children can lead their own learning by making choices about where they want to learn in the environment, what they need to use and who they need to help them.	■ Resources will be displayed in a way which enables children to access them independently. ■ Resources will be labelled so that children will know what is available to them. ■ We will model how to use resources and equipment (where appropriate) so that children can get the most from the opportunities available to them. ■ Children will be given support to make their own plans and the language to communicate what they want to do, where they want to do it and with whom. ■ Adults will intervene sensitively so that they enhance, not disrupt, children's play.

On page 10 there are some more examples of 'WHAT we would expect to see if we were successful', this time for the part of our purpose that is focused on highly skilled staff.

Again, bear in mind, that this list is not exhaustive. Going through this process together with your staff will ensure that we explore each area in depth, that everyone contributes, everyone has a voice and there is a real dialogue about what is important.

This builds relationships, helps us to understand where our team members are coming from and will develop a shared understanding of how we are going to achieve our purpose.

Our purpose	
To provide children with high quality environments and highly skilled staff that can support them to explore and learn about the world around them.	
How?	**What?**
We need staff who demonstrate a rounded knowledge of pedagogy and practice.	Staff will: ■ Have an in-depth knowledge of child development. ■ Have an in-depth knowledge of how children learn and how we (as adults) can facilitate and support learning. ■ Demonstrate a rounded knowledge of observation, assessment and planning. ■ Have a view on how to construct a learning environment based on sound academic principles/evidenced based-practice. ■ Actively pursue and be supported to continue to develop their knowledge, skills and talents.
We need staff who can identify children's needs and interested, and create opportunities/experiences to meet those needs.	Staff will: ■ Have the ability to make genuine connections with parents/carers to understand what children show that they know, understand and can do at home. ■ Have the ability to make genuine connections with children so that they feel secure in their environment. ■ Have the ability to listen to children and ensure that their thoughts, feelings and interests are represented in planning, play and the environment. ■ Have the ability to intervene sensitively to support/scaffold play and effectively identify 'teachable moments'. ■ Have the ability to work as part of a team to meet children's needs. ■ Have the ability to plan opportunities and experiences that continue to help children to develop their skills, knowledge and talents. ■ Have the ability to identify what children know, understand and can do so that adults, the environment and activities continue to offer challenge. ■ Have the ability to identify and take appropriate action to support the needs of vulnerable children.

You may be wondering why I haven't completed a WHY, HOW and WHAT document for you. The answer is that every setting is different; the values, beliefs, qualifications, personal experiences and the communities that we serve will differ from one setting to another, therefore our WHY, HOW and WHAT will be deeply personal to everyone involved. That is why it is important to try and include as many of our team members as possible. The more of our team that we are able to involve, the deeper the level of understanding and ownership. If you don't own something, it's much harder (but not impossible) to care about it.

On your journey together there are likely to be two additional benefits:

- firstly, you will find out things that you did not know about your staff members,
- secondly, your journey as a team will set you apart from other settings, and as you are on your way you will develop things that are unique to your organisation (possibly a unique selling point) which may just separate you from all the other settings around you and give you a competitive edge.

Task 4 – WHY, HOW and WHAT

Using the template at Annex A, you should now feel confident to build your WHY, HOW and WHAT with your team.

Remember:

- Your WHAT/outcomes for success also need to be generated for financial planning, marketing and complying with legislative requirements etc. These wider topics are not something that need to be done will your team. You, therefore, may choose to work as a team to unpick what needs to happen in practice, but choose to work with more senior members of staff when looking at legislation, financial planning etc.

- We are still not at the stage where we can identify actions. Your WHAT statements will define how you know that something is in place and working well.

"The essence of strategy is choosing what not to do."
Michael Porter, Professor at the Harvard Business School and world renown strategist in management, business and competitiveness.

If you are thinking…'Why can't I just use what's in the Early Years Inspection Handbook as a framework for my monitoring and evaluation activities?' That's a fair and valid question.

- If we **just** use the Ofsted inspection framework, we will always be making changes to what we do and how we do it because our monitoring and evaluation system won't be anchored to our WHY, HOW and WHAT.

- The private, voluntary and independent sector is complex because its settings are both educational establishments and businesses. Ofsted is only ever going to be interested in the impact that our provision has on the development of children, so, if our monitoring and evaluation systems only focus on this element, the business side of things could suffer which could lead to sustainability issues, staffing crises and problems in complying with wider legislation etc.

- If we have a systematic approach to developing our monitoring and evaluation activities, we will only ever be doing what is needed to ensure that what we do is effective. Over the years, I have seen countless monitoring systems that have been built on Ofsted inspection frameworks and in many of those settings, the leadership team just keeps adding to what they do when the framework changes, rather than looking at what is important and necessary. As a result, there are leaders and managers out there that feel completely bogged down by paperwork and unnecessarily complex systems. The worst of it is, they are frightened to stop doing anything in case it affects their next Ofsted inspection!

Understanding the importance of and need for a robust business strategy is, therefore, crucial not only to help us deal with the ever-changing world in which we live but to help us to maintain our sanity. Our monitoring and evaluation systems will develop from the things that are important to our business, and they will help us to work smarter not harder.

The good news is that you will never have to create your system from scratch ever again. From now on you will only ever need to review and amend your business strategy. Your HOW and your outcomes for success will need to be reviewed annually to ensure that they remain fit for purpose and the entirety of your business strategy – your WHY, HOW and WHAT will need to be reviewed when there are significant changes to legislation/ policy/ finance or a change in circumstances such as an unexpected 'inadequate' grading. When there aren't any significant factors to consider, your business strategy only need be reviewed every 3 years.

Turning outcomes for success into actions

By now our business strategy is likely to look a little like this (see example of action mapping below) so, the next step in the process is to identify the actions that we need to take.

I have started to number each section so that I can keep track of what belongs where. As we look down the list of WHATS, it becomes immediately apparent that we need the detail that sits underneath our WHAT to know how to put this into practice and to ensure that this part of our work has been carried out to a high standard.

If you are working through this process and are about to throw in the towel because you have lots of sheets of paper, **don't**!

You haven't done anything wrong ! You have just designed an entire business strategy – something that usually takes new businesses months to establish. It is an incredibly complex and time-consuming piece of work, but I can guarantee that the rewards will be worth it.

Example of action mapping

	Our purpose			
No.	**How?**	**Nos**	**What?**	**Actions**
1.	We need to provide well-resourced environments both inside and outside which enable us to deliver a broad and balanced curriculum.	1.1	The 7 areas of learning will be well represented in our resources and equipment.	
		1.2	There will be a range of open-ended resources across our environments.	
		1.3	Our environments and resources will be representative of the communities we serve.	
2.	We need to provide environments that are safe for children to explore and investigate.	2.1	The indoor environment will be secure.	
		2.2	The outdoor environment will be secure.	
		2.3	All adults will be suitable to work with children.	

The list of 'WHATS' in the table is clearly not comprehensive of all areas needing attention, and it will depend on the individual setting.

Lots of people have asked me how long the process will take from the development of their WHY to a comprehensive list of actions. As someone who works with this framework regularly, I can take a full team of staff from their WHY to actions in two days, but that is with a firm hand on the rudder and a strict schedule. For someone who is working through this process with their team for the first time, realistically it is going to take around 6 days, likely to be spread across several staff meetings or development days. The process has however been broken down into manageable chunks to cover the WHY, HOW, WHAT and actions in a way that is meaningful for your staff team. As a rule of thumb, the whole process should be completed within 3-4 months. You can shortcut the process by reducing the number of people taking part (i.e. just senior leaders or the deputy), but this **will** reduce the wealth of contributions from your team and you will have to find alternative strategies to communicate your messages to ensure that everyone is on the same page.

THINK ABOUT...

If you are feeling a little overwhelmed by all of your outcomes for success (WHATs), break them down into sections and distribute a section to each team member. Think about who would be best placed to look at a particular section? Are there staff members who have strengths in specific areas? If you want to ensure that you have a really broad range of actions, try assigning the same section to 2 members of staff, but do not ask them to develop the actions together. By asking them to complete the task separately you are likely to end up with a more rounded view of what needs to be done as each person may think of different things.

In the example below, I have taken one of our WHATs and begun to develop a set of actions.

Example of action mapping (with examples of actions)

No.	How?	Nos	What?	Actions
			Our purpose	
2.	We need to provide environments that are safe for children to explore and investigate.	2.1	Secure intdoor environment	
		2.2	Secure outdoor environment	
		2.3	All adults suitable to work with children.	■ Seek references for all prospective members of staff. ■ Ensure that references come from a valid source and not a friend, neighbour or family member. ■ Ensure that each new member of staff has undertaken a DBS and associated checks (including health) before they start to work with children to reduce the risk of an unsuitable adult working with children. ■ Require all staff to move to the DBS update service at the next point of renewal or at the point of employment. ■ Log onto the DBS update service each term to check that individual circumstances have not changed. ■ Issue a 6 monthly health and suitability declaration form to staff. ■ Ensure that supervision/1-to-1 discussions about performance focus on each member of staff's health, well-being, change in circumstances and anything that may affect their ability to undertake their role and responsibilities. ■ Ensure that formal supervisions/1-to-1 discussions happen at least once a term for all members of staff. ■ Ensure that all members of staff understand the Whistleblowing policy.

THINK ABOUT...

Devising actions for all of your WHATs will be time-consuming. You, therefore, need to be realistic about how long it is going to take you to complete this piece of work. You need to set yourself a realistic deadline for completion because if this part of the process is rushed, your monitoring framework will suffer.

You also need to ensure that staff are not documenting every action that they can possibly think of. We need actions that directly link to our WHAT/outcomes for success. This is not the place for minute details.

Task 5. – Developing your actions

It's finally time to develop a set of actions against each one of your outcomes for success. Each of your WHATs is going to need unpicking to establish a robust set of actions to ensure that practice is of the highest quality. There are two things that you should be aware of - firstly, if this task is left to one person, they are likely to feel overwhelmed, and through no fault of their own, they are also likely to miss critical actions. It is, therefore, advisable to ask other members of staff to support the process; by having more people to review particular sections you can work through your list of WHATs more quickly and with 2 or more people looking at the same section you are likely to ensure that you develop a more comprehensive list of actions.

However, you will need to explain the task in detail to staff; it is easy for staff to refer to what they do rather than thinking about all the possible actions that could come out of a statement so, you will need to think about how you will encourage staff to logically unpick each section. Secondly, unpicking each of your WHATs will take time, even when you are including others, therefore, you need to give yourself plenty of time to complete this part of the process in detail. Rushing to meet a deadline may have a significant impact on the overall quality of your monitoring and self-evaluation framework. It may be more helpful to develop a section at a time.

Mapping your actions against the EYFS

Once we feel that we have a thorough set of WHAT statements (or outcomes for success) and we have a comprehensive list of actions, it is time to get out the EYFS statutory framework again (or whatever legal framework you use to shape what you do with children) and to tick off the things that have already been covered. My prediction is that if you have spent time unpicking your WHY, HOW and WHAT rigorously, your actions will go into far more depth than the statements in the EYFS. This means that you will be working well beyond the minimum requirements of the legal framework.

Reviewing your actions against the EYFS at this point will also ensure that nothing has been overlooked.

Developing meaningful roles and responsibilities

With our WHY, HOW, WHAT and our actions established, we now have sound foundations on which to base our roles and responsibilities.

Although many settings will already have a team in place with defined roles and responsibilities, the framework that we have just created will provide us with an opportunity to look in more depth at where actions/ tasks should sit within our setting and whether each of the established roles is contributing fully to what we do.

Each of the actions/tasks that we've identified are important and will need to be assigned to someone, but the key question is 'at what level should each task be undertaken?'

Setting actions/tasks to the right level

To make the most of this opportunity, we need to put what staff already do and what we know about our staff team to one side and focus solely on the framework that we have created. We need to think about the level that an action/task should sit at, rather than naming a person at this stage.

If we start to allocate actions based on a person, things get messy as we start to think about what practitioners are capable of, i.e. what they are good at and more crucially, what they are not good at. This is likely to mean that the distribution of tasks is uneven, that tasks are allocated on the basis of personality rather than function and that we may inadvertently load ourselves (as leaders and managers) with more activities because we feel that individuals in our organisation haven't got enough knowledge, experience or that they simply are not capable.

We need to think about the level of skill, experience and knowledge we would expect staff to hold at different levels of our organisation – so, what would we expect anyone working as a practitioner, a room leader or a deputy manager to be able to do? And, ultimately what should they know?

Consider if your roles build in term of levels of responsibility. For example, a room leader may have the same actions/tasks as a practitioner, but they may also have responsibilities for monitoring staff and reviewing the quality and accuracy of observations, assessments and learning journals. Is there a difference in the level of responsibility that unqualified members of staff hold compared to qualified staff members?

Depending on the structure of your organisation you may have as few as 3 levels through to as many as 7 (usually seen in nursery chains).

Those levels may look something like this:

- L1 Practitioners
- L2 Room leaders
- L3 Deputy manager /SENDCo/ Designated Lead for Safeguarding
- L4 Manager
- L5 Committee/Proprietor/Director/ Area Manager

Or

- L1 Practitioners
- L2 Middle leaders (room leaders, SENDCo and Designated Safeguarding Lead)
- L3 Management (Manager and Deputy)

There is no right or wrong way to approach this. It will depend on how each setting/organisation is structured and our view of where responsibilities should sit. As we work through our list, we will need to identify at what level each action should sit.

> **THINK ABOUT…**
>
> Redefining responsibilities should not be undertaken with the whole staff team because it is highly sensitive and the slightest hint that we are looking at where actions/tasks sit within our setting could send negative ripples across our team and create uncertainty. You may, however, wish to include senior managers to gain a more rounded and balanced view.

The frequency of tasks

How often actions need to take place is also important as this has an impact on workload. If a particular level only has a handful of actions but those actions need to happen day in, day out, and they aren't quick tasks, adding additional responsibilities may tip the workload for that level to unrealistic proportions unless there are lots of people working at that level to share tasks amongst. Mapping out actions this way will also enable you to plan non-contact time at the different levels. If we are expecting room leaders/middle leaders to sample children's records for accuracy and the appropriateness of next steps, they will need dedicated time to do this as staff will find it difficult to perform this task well whilst they are in ratio.

We also need to think about the management level of work. If we continue to assign tasks to our own management level because we are concerned that we are burdening staff or that staff have not got the knowledge or skill to carry out the task, our own workload is likely to be disproportionately large. This could indicate that we aren't providing enough opportunities within our setting for staff to grow and develop, which may hinder our ability to fill vacancies, as and when they arise.

The time allocated to tasks

Working out how long a task should take is an important part of looking at the frequency of tasks and the overall workload of a level. We need to think carefully about what is involved in the task so that we don't underestimate the time needed to carry it out effectively. This may on occasions mean that we need to talk to staff about what a task may involve if we are not sure.

Once we have mapped out where tasks/actions should sit and their frequency, we can use the framework over the page to review the current responsibilities of staff.

There are two reasons why we might want to do this.

1. We have established that the world of early years is ever changing, which has an impact on what we expect of our staff at different levels of our organisation. Those changes often happen in a disconnected and fragmented way as we are usually responding to a change in legislation.

We will, therefore, be tempted to:
   a. implement new responsibilities or new ways of working without reviewing the whole of a role,
   b. we may give someone responsibility for something because they have more capacity in their day at that point in time,
   c. we may give ourselves the task because it is something that needs to be done quickly etc.

This is likely to mean that over time, task and responsibilities end up sitting at the wrong level, workloads vary considerably, and job descriptions become out of date. Undertaking a review of levels of responsibility will help to ensure that workloads remain manageable and doable.

2. If you have inherited a setting with a mixed history of success, you may find that job descriptions no longer bear any resemblance to the job that staff members are doing. This could have an impact on how individual staff members are interpreting their role, and may mean that some staff members are doing far more than others. We may, therefore, wish to use our actions list to carefully craft a new set of roles and responsibilities.

It is important to remember that you need to take legal advice if you intend to make significant changes to job descriptions or if you find that your staff haven't got a job description! There may be legal implications around contracts and length of service and staff members are likely to have specific employment rights.

The format we use to map actions to levels and frequency is unimportant, as long as we develop a clear picture of what should be happening, where and how often, across our staff team. The following provides examples of how you may wish to capture this information in case you are unsure where to start.

Examples of how to map actions against levels of responsibility (use of level)

Actions	Management Level √	Management Level Notes	Middle Leader Level √	Middle Leader Level Notes	Practitioners Level √	Practitioners Level Notes
■ Log into DBS update service each term to check that individual circumstances have not changed.	√	½ a day a term as most staff are now on the update service.				
■ Regularly produce observations and assessments for each child which captures what children know, understand and can do.			√	On-going process. Observations and assessments generated whilst working with children.	√	On-going process. Observations and assessments generated whilst working with children.
■ Check the accuracy of observation and assessments.	√	½ a day a term sampling children's records for accuracy, moderating the judgements made by staff and their team leaders.	√	½ a day a term sampling children's records for accuracy, appropriate next steps and to ensure that records are up-to-date.		

Examples of how to map actions against levels of responsibility (with reference to post)

Actions	Manager		Deputy		Practitioners	
	√	Notes	√	Notes	√	Notes
■ Log into DBS update service each term to check that individual circumstances have not changed.	√	About ¼ of a day a term as most staff are now on update service.				
■ Regularly produce observations and assessments for each child which capture what children know, understand and can do.			√	On-going process. Observations and assessments generated whilst working with children.	√	On-going process. Observations and assessments generated whilst working with children.
■ Check the accuracy of observation and assessments.	√	½ a day every other term sampling children's records for accuracy, appropriate next steps and moderating the judgements made by staff.	√	½ a day every other term sampling children's records for accuracy, appropriate next steps and moderating the judgements made by staff. (Manager one term, Deputy the next).		

I have created a notes column to record how often activities should happen and to provide myself with a bit of a rationale for my thinking in the two examples provided, however, this is down to personal choice.

The first example illustrates the use of levels within an organisation. This is likely to be a better solution for larger setting, whereas the **second example refers to posts**. The approach remains the same in both cases, but smaller settings may wish to use roles rather than levels due to smaller staff numbers.

If you are starting with roles, you will need to keep reminding yourself that this is not about the person currently in that role, it is about the level of responsibility assigned to that role.

Task 6. – Mapping actions against levels of responsibility

You can now start to assign actions to different levels of responsibility within your organisation (and if it helps, you will find a template for this at Annex B). It does not matter how many levels you have within your organisation, or how small your setting is, the process is exactly the same. What we are mapping is what it is reasonable to expect people to be able to do at the different levels of your organisation.

Now compare this information to the current responsibilities of your staff team. Are there changes that you need to make to even out workload? Is everyone making a significant contribution to your organisation?

Once you have completed this part of the process, you will have produced a robust framework that will underpin your monitoring and evaluation activities.

Chapter 2: Developing an effective monitoring framework

If you are a leader, manager, proprietor, part of a board of trustees, a deputy, a room leader or have an aspect of your job that requires you to check out whether something is in place and working well, you have a role that contributes to the governance of your setting or organisation.

Governance is all around us; from the highest levels of government to small companies with only a couple of employees. The problem is that we don't really talk about governance in early years, or see what we do as being part of a structure that governs our setting or organisation and if we're not talking about it, we're certainly not putting systems in place to ensure that governance is effective!

Understanding Governance

The term governance at its most basic refers to:
- the processes we design to ensure that our organisation and staff are accountable/answerable to someone for the actions we take,
- the open and transparent ways in which our organisation operates,
- the way we comply with any legislation/regulations that apply to us
(UNESCO, 2017)

and as companies in receipt of public funding (i.e. the nursery education grant), we should be operating in the best interests of the communities that we serve.

The 'what' we are accountable for is driven by the purpose of our business, how our business is constituted and the ethos and culture that we create around our purpose or WHY.

Why am I telling you this?
Effective monitoring and evaluation systems are part of our governance structure and if we don't create solid foundations, at some point the cracks will begin to show, maybe not in this inspection, but the next or when there are significant changes to our statutory or inspection frameworks.

In the previous chapter, we explored the creation of a business strategy and if we have implemented the process thus far, we will have started to develop our governance structure.

Through this process, we will have developed a framework that clearly maps why we exist, through to the responsibilities held at each level of the organisation and the contribution that those levels of responsibility make to our WHY. That puts us in the perfect place to start thinking about the development of a monitoring framework.

Before we move on, I ought to clarify why there are separate chapters on monitoring and self-evaluation.

Self-evaluation is what we do when we make judgements based on the evidence that we have and what we know. It, therefore, makes sense to ensure that our sources of evidence are both accurate and reliable before moving on to interpreting what this information tells us about the quality of our provision. Separating out and focusing on our monitoring activities will ensure that we have a sound basis for our decision making when it comes to identifying what we do well and where there is room for improvement.

> "What gets measured, gets done!"
> Peter Drucken, Business consultant, lecturer and author.

As leaders and managers, we are expected to have an accurate view of the quality of our provision, and we know that our understanding of that view will be tested at the point of inspection.

How we come to that understanding will depend on the monitoring activities that we have in place, their frequency, the breadth of things we review as well as and the depth we choose to go to, to unpick if what we do is effective.

It will not be a surprise to know that if our monitoring activities are not robust or effective, the information that they provide is likely to be inaccurate.

If we are then depending on this information to identify our strengths and our areas for development, our view of what is working well and what isn't is likely to be at best skewed or at worse, wrong.

During the time that I have been analysing Ofsted inspection reports, monitoring and self-evaluation has been the most prevalent issue raised in inadequate and requires improvement inspection outcomes, but a little-known fact is that most of the other top trending issues could also be attributed to problems with our monitoring and evaluation systems.

The table below identifies the top ten trending inspection issues for the early years private, voluntary and independent sector for the academic year, September 2017-July 2018.

Inspection Trends for the academic year 2017-2018

Trend No.	Area of Practice	No. of Actions/Recs.	% of Actions/Recs.
1st	Monitoring & Self-Evaluation	368	14%
2nd	Planning & Challenge	278	10.6%
3rd	Management of Staff	266	10.1%
4th	Suitable People	194	7.4%
5th	Safeguarding Knowledge	171	6.5%
6th	Observation, Assessment & Next Steps	137	5.2%
7th	Partnership with Parents	132	5%
8th	Managing Risk	102	3.9%
9th	Information for Ofsted	89	3.4%
Joint 10th	Key Person	83	3.2%
Joint 10th	Managing Behaviour	83	3.2%

Source: Inspection Trends: A Report for the Early Years Private, Voluntary & Independent Sector, Early Years Fundamentals, 2018.

From my own analysis of over 5000 inspection reports and years of anecdotal conversations with leaders and managers, it would seem that early years qualifications have not gone far enough to prepare us to be leaders and managers.

To exemplify this further, I undertook a review of the first 50 under-graduate courses that popped up in a Google search in March 2018. Out of those 50 foundation and full degree programmes, there were only 2 that had mandatory modules in leadership and management and two programmes that specifically focused on leadership in the early years; the rest were focused solely on pedagogy and practice.

In my humble opinion, Government has been so intent on ensuring that practitioners can effectively lead learning that the need for effective governance and leadership has been overlooked in the early years private and voluntary sector. This is not the same in the school sector, where a huge amount of importance has been placed on leadership, so much so that Government created a national professional qualification framework for headteachers, senior leaders and middle leaders known as the NPQH, NPQSL and the NPQML (DfE, 2017 & 2018).

What I still cannot fathom is why Government hasn't made the same provision for existing and aspirant leaders and managers. It would make sense to create a specific strand of the NPQ framework for early years providers or

at least to produce something that reflects the similarities in function across the education sector, but also deals with the complexities of being both a business and an educational provider.

In Annex C, I've compared the inspection issues seen in the early years sector with areas of study found in the NPQ Content and Assessment Framework (DfE, 2017). This mapping exercise will enable you to see how the content of this established framework could contribute to a more knowledgeable and highly skilled early years leadership workforce.

The table in Annex C maps actions and recommendations that have appeared with frequency in *requires improvement* and *inadequate* inspection outcomes against the content of different parts of the NPQ framework. If nothing else, this information provides us with subject areas to focus on so that we can tailor our reading/ professional development toward those missing pieces of our professional development puzzle.

The importance of monitoring

We need to understand that monitoring and self-evaluation frameworks/systems are about control. We need to be in control of what is happening in our setting which requires us to:

- have an accurate and rounded view of the performance of our organisation (and the people in it),
- put systems and processes in place to ensure that things *stay* within our control.

Monitoring activities are the primary source of information used by leaders and manager to determine whether:

- We continue to appropriately identify and address safeguarding concerns so that we can protect the children in our care,
- We continue to provide environments that are safe both physically and emotionally for our children and our staff,
- We continue to comply with legislation,
- We continue to be inclusive,
- We are developing and maintaining respectful relationships with parents, carers and external professionals to maximise the effectiveness of learning and development opportunities,

- The activities and opportunities that we offer continue to be well matched to the individual learning, development and care needs of our children,
- All children continue to make good progress over the time that they are with us,
- All children continue to receive an appropriate level of challenge to ensure that each child makes the best progress they can,
- Staff have the knowledge and skills to deliver a broad and balanced curriculum,
- We continue to grow the knowledge, talents and skills of our practitioners so that they are not only effective in role, but that they are able to support and mentor others within our setting and/or move into more senior roles,
- We continue to fill our places term on term,
- We continue to bring in enough income to at least cover the running costs of our business,
- Our service users (parents, carers and children) continue to be happy with the services that they receive.

The most important word here is 'continue'. What lets many settings down is that:

- monitoring activities do not happen with consistency (and in some cases, some activities may have completely dropped off the radar all together),
- monitoring activities are not extensive enough to ensure that all aspects of the business are working well,
- self-evaluation is inaccurate and/or out-of-date,
- plans to develop areas of practice are not exhaustive enough (we deal with the visible problem rather than the underlying cause.

all of which points to the fact that monitoring and self-evaluation systems are not robust or effective. This means that leaders and managers are unlikely to have an accurate view of the quality of their provision, the competence of their staff, their financial position, the views of their service users or their current and projected occupancy levels. Each of these issues could have devasting consequences for a setting. The impact could be sustainability issues, failure to comply with legislation and the possibility that those with regulatory responsibilities (Ofsted, Local Authority Safeguarding Services, the Health and Safety Executive and the Information Commissioner's Office etc.) could find something that we did not know about, which, in turn, could lead to financial penalties, prosecution or forced closure.

By now you will have noticed that I've used the words 'monitoring framework' several times. This is because we need to understand the totality of what needs to be monitored in order to make informed decisions about what is important, what's not and what can be parked when life sends challenges that require our undivided attention.

Monitoring activities need to be both logical and systematic if they are to work effectively. That means identifying what we need to review, how often, at what level that activity should take place (practitioner, room leader, management team) and any criteria that will help us to make consistent judgements about the effectiveness of what we do (Mullins, 2016).

How do you know what to monitor?

In Chapter 1, we have identified a list of actions or things that need to happen for our 'outcomes for success' or our WHAT to be met. We now need to look at that list again to identify the actions that need to be reviewed/monitored to ensure that they happen with consistency and to the standard that we require.

Our list of actions is likely to be rather large, so we need to put a system in place that will help us to prioritise them, identifying areas that are of critical importance to our business first.

As we run down our list, we need to assess the level of risk or likely consequences associated with not carrying out an action or not doing it well. We need to ask ourselves, what is the worst-case scenario if:

- This did not happen at all/was not in place?
- Did not happen with consistency?
- Was not effective?

To help us work out those risks, we need to think about:

- The impact on the services that we deliver. Would they still be effective or delivered to the standard that we require? Could we still deliver high quality opportunities and experiences that would meet the needs of all children?
- Would this reduce our ability to safeguard children or have an impact on the effectiveness of our safeguarding arrangements?

- Would this damage our reputation with our service users?
- Would we still be meeting legal requirements?
- Would this damage our relationship with our staff team or individual team members?
- Would this damage our relationship with our trustees or committee members?
- Would we still be able to generate income? / Would we still be able to meet our running costs?

(Mind Tools, 2018.)

There may be other factors that you want to consider when you are assessing the risks which may have come from your WHY and HOW.

Below, is an example of risk mapping which has been populated with a small number of common actions that many settings will undertake. You do not need to use this format, but if you find it helpful, you will find a template for this approach at Annex D.

You may not necessarily agree with the level of risk that I have assigned to each of these actions, but this is unimportant. It's the process of managing risk that is important. Our own experiences, both good and bad will influence our thinking; good experiences tend to make people less risk averse, whereas bad experiences will usually make us slightly more cautious. How we judge

Example of how to map risk

Actions	Low	Medium		High		What is my rationale for the level of risk?
	1	2	3	4	5	
Seek references for all prospective members of staff.					X	Prospective members of staff may be the current focus of a safeguarding investigation or may have resigned before the management team was able to initiate an investigation. We are therefore unable to say that staff members are suitable to work with children if references are not carried out.
Ensure that references come from a valid source and not a friend, neighbour or family member.					X	Individuals have been known to fake references or use family members to gain employment, particularly if they left their previous employment under a cloud. We are, therefore, unable to say that the staff member is suitable to work with children if this is not carried out.
Sample children's records for accuracy, appropriate next steps and to ensure that records are up-to-date.					X	Our core business is meeting the needs of children. If the observations and assessments made by staff are inaccurate or not kept up-to-date, staff are unlikely to be meeting the needs of all children. This will affect children's progress and our ability to identify and intervene early when children are experiencing difficulties. It could also mean that we miss early safeguarding indicators.
Send out a termly newsletter to parents.	X					As long as we maintain our various other activities (parent evenings, our parents' news board, making time to meet with parents at the beginning and end of the day etc.) there should be a low impact if we are unable to produce a newsletter.
Ensure that all staff members have an advanced level of safeguarding training.			X			In an ideal world, we would want to ensure that all staff have as much safeguarding knowledge and training as possible to be able to identify and raise concerns at the earliest opportunity. Time and funding makes this difficult to achieve, therefore, we will manage this situation by ensuring that there are several members of staff who have the depth of knowledge and skills to support the whole staff team. This will ensure that we can continue to respond swiftly and appropriately to safeguarding concerns.

risk will also be heavily influenced by our level and depth of knowledge of early years pedagogy and practice, business strategy, legislation and our understanding of risk management. I have used 5 levels of risk to help me to prioritise my long list of actions, but you may choose to use 3 - low, medium and high.

You may not feel it necessary to write a rationale for your levels of risk and may feel comfortable just talking through any issues or concerns with other members of staff or senior leaders. I use a column for rationale to help me prioritise tasks within a risk category. When there are large numbers of high level risks it is helpful to understand those that are more pressing than others.

Task 7. – Risk Mapping

Working with your management/leadership team, assign levels of risk to the actions that you created against your WHY, HOW and WHAT. It is entirely up to you how you define your levels of risk, you may just choose high, medium and low rather than the 5 levels shown in the example on the previous page. What matters is that you start to separate important actions from things that are less important. This will form the basis of your monitoring framework and will ensure that:

- There is a reason for all monitoring activities,
- You focus on the things that will make the most difference to your business and practice,
- The volume of monitoring activities remains manageable.

Once we have assessed levels of risk against all of our actions it is easy to order them from the highest to lowest. The actions that carry the highest levels of risk need to be at the very top of our list.

Having done this, it is likely that we will still have a considerable number of actions that will carry a high risk. It, therefore, makes sense to order all these actions in terms of their importance. Previously, we used the questions in order of importance (highlighted opposite) to consider the consequences of not carrying out an action,

but these criteria will now need to be placed in order of importance to help us create a manageable framework. I have put 'safeguarding children' as my top priority, which will be closely followed by the need to meet 'legal requirements' and then the need to 'generate income'.

Questions in order of importance
1. Would this reduce our ability to safeguard children or have an impact on the effectiveness of our safeguarding arrangements?
2. Would we still be meeting the legal requirements?
3. Would we still be able to generate income / meet our running costs?

How you prioritise your list is entirely up to you. There are no right or wrong answers because the things that are most important to you will be driven by your WHY.

However, legal requirements will need to be towards the top of your list. It is also not unheard of for companies to think about income generation first, because without it, they would cease to exist.

THINK ABOUT...

It is far easier to assign a level of risk to each action and then to look at all the actions in that level together and to place them in order of importance. Even within the high-risk category, there will be things that need to take priority over others.

Every action that we deem to be important is worthy of monitoring. If not doing something is likely to have a negative impact on our business or practice, we need to make sure that it not only happens, but, at the same time that it is effective.

As we look down our list of actions (which starts with those that carry the highest risk) there will be some items that only ever need to happen once, items that just require a quick check, whilst others which will require a more in-depth approach to ensure that what is happening is working well.

We, therefore, need to think about separating actions into two main columns; one for quick checks and the other which will focus on the actual effectiveness of the actions.

This task will be easier if we first scan down the list and pick out any actions that are also monitoring activities. For example, one of my actions was to check the accuracy of observation and assessments.

Clearly, this is a monitoring activity that would ensure the effectiveness of the observations and assessments carried out by practitioners.

We can, therefore, move this action into our in-depth monitoring column, which can be seen in the two examples opposite.

Once we have a definitive list of actions in order of risk and importance, we have the blueprint for our monitoring framework. It will have taken time and effort to get here, but we now have a document that provides a rationale for what we do, why we do it and how important each action is in helping us to achieve our outcomes for success.

"If you can't measure it, you can't improve it!"
Lord Kelvin, Professor of mathematics and physics who developed the Kelvin scale of temperature measurement.

Task 8. – Ordering your risks

Now that you have a clear view of your high to low risk actions, you can order them in terms of priority. Start with your high-risk category first and place them in order of importance. You should feel that the level of risk decreases the further you get down your list. You may find it helpful to use the questions we identified previously to determine how important an action is:

- The impact on the services that we deliver. Would they still be effective or delivered to the standard that we require? Could we still deliver high quality opportunities and experiences that would meet the needs of ALL of our children?

- Would this reduce our ability to safeguard children or have an impact on the effectiveness of our safeguarding arrangements?
- Would this damage our reputation with our service users?
- Would we still be meeting the legal requirements?
- Would this damage our relationship with our staff team or individual team members?
- Would this damage our relationship with our Board of Trustees or Committee Members?
- Would we still be able to generate income? / Would we still be able to meet our running costs?
(Mind Tools, 2018.)

Example of risk mapping

Actions	Low	Medium		High		What is my rationale for the level of risk?
	1	2	3	4	5	
Regularly produce observations and assessments for each child which capture what children know, understand and can do.					X	Staff need to be able to identify what children know, understand and can do to provide opportunities and experiences that continue to build on their knowledge, skills and understanding. Without regular observations and assessments, staff will not be able to plan for the needs of their key children.
Check the accuracy of observation and assessments.					X	Our core business is meeting the needs of children. If the observations and assessments made by staff are inaccurate or not kept up-to-date, staff are unlikely to be meeting the needs of all children. This is likely to affect children's progress and our ability to identify and intervene early when children are experiencing difficulties. It could also mean that we miss early safeguarding indicators.

Example of how to identify the type of monitoring actvitiy

Actions	What type of monitoring needs to take place?		Expectations for practice/criteria/standard
	A quick check that this has been done	In-depth (What needs to be monitored)	How will we judge the effectiveness of practice? (What we will look for or at)
Log into the DBS update service each term to check that individual circumstances have not changed.	Yes	N/A	
Regularly produce observations and assessments for each child which capture what children know, understand and can do.	N/A	Check the accuracy of observation and assessments.	

Task 9. – Identifying what type of monitoring is needed

You should now be in a good position to identify the type of monitoring activity required to ensure that actions have happened or that they continue to be effective. Use a format that you feel comfortable with as there is no prescribed way of doing this, but if you wish to use the template in the example above, you will find it at Annex E.

Setting your monitoring criteria

Our monitoring framework is nearly complete. The only things left to do are to identify how we will judge the effectiveness of practice, the frequency of those activities and who should have the responsibility to carry them out.

Monitoring criteria or expectations for practice are important because they enable us to consistently judge the accuracy, effectiveness and/or consistency of what we do. However, we need to be clear in our minds about what we intend to look for and at. Only when we have identified criteria, drawn up a set of expectations or have defined what 'good' looks like, will we be able to consistently make a judgement about what staff do and how well they do it.

We need to establish what we will be looking for and at, for several reasons:

1. Monitoring criteria/expectations for practice need to be open, transparent and understood by our staff team. Only when all staff members understand what it is that we are using to judge the effectiveness of practice and performance will they be able to rise to the challenges set.
2. Understanding what the management team expects builds trust. When we are not clear about what it is that we are looking at or for, staff members can become anxious and stressed, feeling like they are being tested for an exam they haven't studied for.
3. Any member of staff (in theory) should be able to pick up a set of criteria or expectations for practice and know what is expected. This will go a long way towards ensuring that there is a consistent and standardised approach to practice and to specific monitoring activities, no matter who carries them out.
4. If all staff members understand the criteria used to assess practice, we have a greater pool of people to support us with our monitoring activities.

Writing down our expectations means that our vision of what good practice looks like and the standards that we wish our teams to reach can be shared, explained and understood by all. The same criteria can also be used to assess the performance of staff. Monitoring is, therefore, fair and transparent.

THINK ABOUT...

Where practice is at its best, the manager will either sit with their staff team to talk about monitoring criteria/the expectations for practice, or team members will be invited to construct the criteria together with the management team. This is a powerful way of working as it ensures that everyone involved has a consistent understanding of what will be reviewed, why and the implications for practice.

Sometimes our expectations for practice don't go far enough to explain what we need to see or what needs to happen, so we may wish to introduce examples of W.A.G.O.L.L. to our staff team. W.A.G.O.L.L. is the acronym for 'What A Good One Looks Like'. They are often a quick way to communicate our expectations and reduce the need to write down lengthy explanation. They can be documents that we have produced ourselves, or we can choose W.A.G.O.L.L. examples from the documents and files produced by our practitioners. The beauty of these examples is that they can be included in your staff handbook or induction materials, so staff are always aware of the standards that have been set for practice. Once your W.A.G.O.L.L.s have been shared you can then use their key features to create your monitoring criteria. For example, this is a good observation of a child; this is what makes it good etc…

Task 10. – Setting criteria for monitoring activities

To ensure a consistent approach to monitoring activities you will need to build a range of criteria. This isn't likely to be a quick task, so you will need to prioritise the activities that would most benefit from monitoring criteria such as observations of adult: child interacts.

Earlier, I shared the example of 'how to create a rigorous and manageable monitoring framework' which also contains a column to identify the criteria you wish staff to use. You will find this at Annex E.

Anyone looking at our list of actions would be forgiven for feeling a little overwhelmed. After all, we have put absolutely everything we do under a microscope and dissected it to make sure that we offer the highest quality services to our children and the communities we serve. What we have produced is both a business strategy and a comprehensive monitoring framework. This means that we will only ever be doing what is needed because we have identified what is important to our setting. However, the prospect of implementing such a huge framework can be more than a little daunting. So, what's the answer?

Three words: create leadership capacity!

> *"Quality is everyone's responsibility."*
> *W. Edwards Deming, Academic and business consultant*
> *best known for his work on Total Quality Management.*

Creating leadership opportunities

Being 'the boss' or the person that everyone looks to in an organisation comes with incredible responsibility. In times gone by, workplaces were dictatorships in which management figures would issue their edicts from on high and the rest of us would dutifully carry them out without question.

Although power and authority still sits with those at the top of our organisation, we now have a much better understanding of leadership and how to get the most from the people that we work with. Modern day leadership books are brimming with strategies to improve our relationship with our staff team, ways to harness potential and the importance of creating leadership opportunities throughout our organisation.

Those books talk of team ownership, about the need for individuals to connect with organisational objectives and for everyone to take responsibility for the quality of what they do.

We may have read many such books or articles, but how we feel about our role and our team will determine how successful we are at creating leadership opportunities and more importantly, leadership capacity.

Distributing leadership tasks and roles across our team (where appropriate) can make a significant impact on the performance of both individual team members and our setting. It can, however, be a frightening thought as we may think that we will lose power and/or control of our setting if we give someone else leadership responsibilities. We can worry about what staff members may think of us if they find out that we don't have as much knowledge as they do about a specific area of practice, and it can create doubts in our minds about our leadership abilities – 'what if they are a better leader than I am?'

These kinds of fears have led to some leaders/managers going to extraordinary lengths to keep 'control' of their staff teams. Some of the worst examples I've seen are:

- managers that insist on going to every possible training session and then 'cherry picking' what is fed back to staff because they believe that they need to have more knowledge than their team members,
- managers who insist on mentoring and coaching staff in subjects they know little about because they do not want anyone else in their setting to support staff,
- managers who create huge workloads for themselves because they refuse to give staff what they perceive to be tasks or responsibilities that carry power or management responsibilties.

The sad thing is that this could not be further from the truth.

Being all things to all people is exhausting and is not sustainable in the long term. Managers who adopt these ways of working put themselves in an impossible position because they create situations where staff will always look to them for answers and guidance. This is a risky strategy for two reasons. Firstly, staff will not have the confidence to work autonomously, which means that a great deal of the manager's time will be taken up with conversations that staff already know the answer to. Secondly, no-one is a subject matter expert in everything, so at some point the manager is not going to be able to give staff the support and advice that they need. Where this is the case, it invariably means that the manager is doing lots of things, but none of them particularly well.

Managers who have fallen prey to this way of thinking need to consider the damage their actions could be having on the quality of provision and on their staff team. How many important things are dropping off the end of the earth because they haven't got time to do all the things that they set themselves? How many staff members are frustrated because their needs continue to be overlooked? Work may be building up around them, but staff aren't 'allowed' to help, therefore, the team's workload is low whilst the manager's is completely off the scale.

Our teams do not need an all-seeing, all-knowing being.

We need to be leaders who can play to the strengths of our team, supporting individuals to develop their knowledge and skills, so that they can lead the development of aspects of practice and contribute to monitoring activities. If we think that leadership is something that only applies to those working in the most senior positions within our organisation, we will lose our ability to make best use of the strengths and potential held within our staff team. Our role as a leader/manager is, therefore, to do what we can to support staff to develop their skills, knowledge and talents. By doing this we will grow the leadership capacity of our setting and achieve far more than we ever could on our own (Harris & Lambert, 2003; Harris, 2013).

Over the years I have found this acronym to be a useful reminder of just how powerful distributing leadership tasks can be:

T ogether
E veryone
A chieves
M ore

Everyone has leadership potential, we just need to unlock it and then guide staff members in the direction of our WHY, HOW and WHAT.

Distributed leadership

In my personal experience, distributed leadership is often not well implemented. In many of the settings that I have worked with, people in leadership positions talk about distributed leadership, but what they are really describing is poor delegation. So, here is a quick tip. If you are regularly taking things off your 'to-do' list and handing them out to staff members, that is not distributed leadership, it is poor delegation. It gives the illusion that we are sharing work out amongst team members, but in reality, we are just creating a little head space for ourselves in the short term. It does not help anyone to develop their leadership skills, it does not grow leadership capacity within our organisation, and it does not make staff members feel valued.

Distributed leadership is about utilising leadership expertise at every level of our organisation (Harris, 2014). That means giving individual staff members responsibilities and opportunities to take on pieces of work that they will lead. This new work will typically play to their strengths or help them to develop their

knowledge, skills and talents. This does not mean that we will lose control, in fact, quite the reverse. Our staff member will lead and be accountable for this work and we will retain overall responsibility by monitoring their approach and progress. This will create the time and space for us to focus on more pressing issues or important tasks. We are growing leadership capacity instead of reducing it by doing everything ourselves.

It is worth remembering that some members of staff will require coaching/mentoring, and some may need to access a specific training programme before they will be able to truly rise to the new challenges set. We may, therefore, need to plan in a little extra time to support staff in the early stages, but our patience will be rewarded with additional leadership capacity in the near future.

The impact of distributed leadership

Let's not underestimate the impact that distributed leadership can have on our setting and, in particular, on our own workload:

- With a greater number of people focused on leadership tasks and responsibilties, we will be able to be more responsive to problems, complaints, change or challenges.
- Decisions are made more quickly, as everyone is clear about their level of autonomy and decision-making boundaries. Management are, therefore, not burdened with decisions that could be made by others. This can speed up the turn-around time for important decisions.
- Staff are given a level of autonomy to work in a way that they feel best addresses the needs of the setting/children. This leads to a greater level of initiative being taken by individual staff members together with a greater sense of ownership when contributing to improvements (or the setting's WHY and HOW), and we are likely to see higher levels of morale as staff feel trusted, valued and empowered.
- If more people are involved in our day-to-day monitoring activities, we will have more opportunity to proactively identify weaker areas of practice before they become problematic. We are also likely to encourage/support staff to develop a greater level of knowledge in specific areas. This will enable our monitoring activities to be undertaken at greater depth.

"We do not see things as they are, we see things as we are"
Anaïs Nin, Author and writer best known for the publication of her diaries.

Another good reason for implementing a framework of distributed leadership is to counteract the effects of cognitive biases.

There are a number of biases that can affect our decision-making process. However, one of the most dangerous when carrying out monitoring activities is confirmation bias.

Confirmation bias is so well documented that it now appears in the Encyclopaedia Britannica. It occurs when we consciously or unconsciously look for evidence that confirms our existing belief or understanding.

If we believe that something is in place and working well, it won't take an awful lot to convince us that we are right even though there may be evidence to the contrary. For some reason we seem to block out or ignore opposing views or evidence.

This happens a great deal after an Ofsted inspection. The manager may be upset or confused about the issues that Ofsted have raised because they cannot identify with the information that has been presented to them. In the mind of the manager, they are meeting Ofsted's expectations and they have seen evidence to prove it - but that sadly isn't the case.

The first thing to say is that Ofsted inspectors are human and, therefore, some mistakes are likely to be made during the course of the thousands of inspections that take place over any given year, but for most reports, the view of provision will be accurate based on the information seen and heard on that day.

As you can imagine, confirmation bias can have a significant impact on the effectiveness of our monitoring activities if we are the only ones looking at the evidence. It is, therefore, important for us to involve other members of staff in monitoring activities to make sure that we have a rounded view of practice and that we challenge each other's perception of what we think is in place and working effectively.

Setting monitoring activities to the right level

In Chapter 1, we identified where/at what level our actions/responsibilities should lie within our organisation. The same now needs to be done with our monitoring activities to ensure that we have a rounded view of practice, that we build leadership capacity and that we balance our own workload.

Just as we did with our list of actions, we now need to think about assigning monitoring activities to specific levels or roles within our setting.

The frequency of monitoring activities and time allocation

Whilst we are allocating monitoring activities to roles within our setting, we also need to consider the frequency of those activities. As we established earlier, if we do not regularly monitor what we do and how effective it is, our view of quality can become out of date very quickly.

I am not advocating that most of our time has to be spent monitoring, but we do need to give some thought to how accurate our data will be if we only look at it either annually or bi-annually. Think about how many opportunities will have been missed to make things even better for our children?

Some things will only need to be reviewed annually, or when there are significant changes to legislation such as policies and procedures, whereas tracking data, the accuracy of observations and assessments and the way the environment is presented etc, will need regular attention. Some activities will also need time away from the children (non-contact time) to do them well, which may have an impact on workload planning across our staff team.

THINK ABOUT…

Something to bear in mind - if you are assigning additional or specific responsibilities to members of staff, these may need to be added to their job descriptions.

Task 11. – Mapping monitoring activities against levels of responsibility

It is now time to look at where monitoring activities ought to sit within your organisation. If you need to use a template to do this, use Annex B, and just change the word 'actions' for 'monitoring'.

Mapping actions against levels of responsibility

Levels of responsibility →						
Actions ↓	√	Notes	√	Notes	√	Notes

Once you have finally completed this part of the process, you will have created a robust framework for your monitoring and evaluation activities.

THINK ABOUT...

Do not underestimate the value of developing monitoring criteria with your staff team - it is a powerful way to ensure a consistency of understanding and approach across your staff.

Organising yourself and others

We now have a rigorous framework for our monitoring activities and the frequency of those activities will form our monitoring cycles. This is a phenomenal achievement, but our success will be short-lived if this framework isn't implemented with consistency.

When we are busy, important things can often drop off the radar because we have so much going on in our heads. 'Post-it' notes and 'to-do' lists will only get us so far. It might, therefore, be worthwhile considering software or apps that will help us to manage our setting's workload, for example Trello.

Trello is a free PC download and mobile app that combines the functions of a 'to do' list, action plan, scheduling assistant and monitoring tool.

It enables the user to manage their workload (and that of others) and can be used to break down big pieces of work into bite-sized chunks. It is popular with both large and small firms in industry because it can be used collaboratively; being cloud-based it enables team leaders to monitor progress and assign tasks even when team members are hundreds of miles away. It is, therefore, perfect for small settings right through to large nursery chains.

It enables you to:

- Create a dedicated work space for projects, large pieces of work and day-to-day management tasks,
- Create as many work spaces (or 'boards' as they are known on Trello) to manage all the plates that you are spinning,
- Order and reorder your tasks as necessary or as often as you like, so that you can manage your working day more effectively,
- Invite individual team members or the whole team to join specific pieces of work,
- Create and assign tasks for team members,
- Put a 'watch' marker on certain tasks to make sure that they have been completed by team members (particularly useful when you need to meet deadlines),
- Change the priority of a team member's tasks because something has now become more urgent,
- Schedule when something needs to be done by (each task will alert you when it has not been completed by the deadline assigned),
- Maintain an overview of tasks that have not yet been started, those that are in progress and those that have been completed.

This simple programme will enable you to quickly ascertain what has not been started, what is in progress and what has been done so far, AND you can see where deadlines have not been met. You can also add attachments to tasks so that you can reduce the amount of paperwork in your setting.

More importantly, it has a repeat function that enables you to schedule tasks throughout the year. So, if you struggle with remembering what to do and when to do it, you could simply upload your monitoring activities to Trello and set the repeat function to weekly, monthly, quarterly, bi-annually, annually or for a specific date.

Trello works for me, but other free software options are available that will help you to manage workloads across your setting. It's definitely worth looking around until you find something that works for you.

The EYFS and the Early Years Inspection Handbook

As we know, legislation does not stay the same, so we need to ensure that we understand the implications of any changes, the impact that they will have on our WHY, HOW and WHAT, and that we reshape what we do accordingly.

Sitting under the legislation, will be various frameworks used by the regulatory body to ensure our compliance. These frameworks interpret the legal requirements and break them down into criteria that is then used during an inspection. We must read them, understand them, but not become a slave to them. If we become preoccupied with just meeting inspection criteria, we will limit our potential. If, however, our approach is anchored in research and evidence-based practice, and the formation of our WHY, HOW and WHAT has been thorough, the services that we provide will be of the highest quality.

Understanding the legislation

There is nothing specific in the EYFS that says that we need to have monitoring activities in place, but it is implied throughout. Phrases like 'providers must have effective systems in place' and 'providers must ensure' make clear that activities need to be sustained in order for us to continue to meet the minimum legal requirements.

The Early Years Inspection Handbook, however, is very different and makes explicit references to how we, as leaders and managers, should maintain an accurate view of the quality of our provision through rigorous self-evaluation which is underpinned by effective monitoring systems. The difference between the two is that the EYFS sets out the minimum legal requirements and the Inspection Handbook provides criteria to assess how well we were able to meet them.

Over the years, the key focus of early years inspections has not changed. Providers are required to:

- Keep children safe,
- Meet the individual learning, development and care needs of children,
- Deliver a broad and balanced curriculum,
- Offer inclusive services,
- Work in partnership with parents/carers and external professionals to maximise children's learning and development opportunities and experiences,
- Monitor and evaluate services using the outcome of those activities to drive continuous improvement. (Ofsted, 2018.)

The interpretation of each of these areas, however, has become more sophisticated over time, and our depth of knowledge and skill has had to grow to meet this enhanced level of challenge.

Although we have just been through an incredibly rigorous process to develop our monitoring framework (which should have involved the EYFS), we need to familiarise ourselves with the Early Years Inspection Handbook to ensure that we have not missed anything important.

Chapter 3: Monitoring and managing performance

Performance management is often misunderstood in the early years sector. It tends to be seen as something separate to our monitoring and evaluation system, processes and activities, yet it makes a significant contribution to our understanding of what's working well and what isn't, and if implemented well, performance management will drive continuous improvement.

Staff teams are our most valuable resource and the success of our setting will depend on:

- how well each member of staff fulfils their role and responsibilities,
- our ability to hold open and honest conversations about their specific strengths and/or any weaker areas of practice,
- well defined and understood personal targets that continue to move practice forward,
- our commitment to supporting the development of staff knowledge and skills,
- how engaged staff are in the development of our setting's priorities for improvement,
- how we can nurture talent and skills, so that individual members of staff can take on roles and additional responsibilities that build leadership capacity.

The quality, depth and level of professional challenge posed during our discussions with staff, alongside performance monitoring activities that enable us to understand what staff know, understand and can do are the only way to develop and sustain high quality provision. However, all of the above will be affected if staff members are not clear about their roles, responsibilities and the expectation for practice.

Clarity of roles and responsibilities

Previously, we have explored how to construct roles and responsibilities through the development of a business strategy, however - it is often the case that leaders/managers inherit a structure; the staff are already in place and their roles and responsibilities have been assigned. Because of this, job descriptions/ competencies and expectations for practice are often overlooked in favour of dealing with what we believe to be our most pressing issues.

However, if staff do not understand their roles, responsibilities and the expectations for practice, the problems that we think we've addressed are unlikely to go away.

A crucial piece of advice for any manager is that we need to make sure that our staff understand what is expected of them and that we invest time in explaining what those expectations look like in practice. Failure to do this means that it wouldn't be the 'fault' of the individual member of staff if they are not meeting the standards we've set.

We can tell ourselves that we have done this, but how do we know that we have done it in a way that is accessible to all members of staff? Have we checked that each staff member is clear about the expectations for practice? And do we revisit those expectations throughout the year?

I am not advocating that we spoon-feed staff – life is busy enough without feeling that we need to constantly chase or remind staff to do things, but the importance of ensuring that all staff have a clear understanding of their role is of paramount importance.

This example may help to clarify what I mean.

Local authority advisor: "Ok Vicky, let's talk about how you know that staff can put your policies into practice."

Nursery manager: "I review our policies every year and then I send a copy of the revisions out to the team. New staff members are given a full pack of our policies before they start with us. I always ask staff to read the policies and to sign to say that they have read and understood them, whether they are new to our setting or just looking at a revised policy."

This happens in many settings because it is the most effective way to communicate lots of information to staff in a short space of time, but often, the most important step in communicating our message is missed; we need to check out that everyone understands what they have read or heard, and that there is a consistent understanding of what to do and how to do it across our staff team.

The same issue often occurs when I'm reviewing the effectiveness of safeguarding arrangements. In this type of scenario, the manager assumes that everyone is clear about their roles and responsibilities because the management team talk about safeguarding all the time, but in reality the manager hasn't gone far enough to check out that everyone understands what is being shared with them/asked of them, and that there is a consistency of understanding.

THINK ABOUT...

Find ways to check each member of staff's understanding of policies and of the expectations that you've set for practice. If you don't and they don't meet the standards required, they aren't underperforming, you are! We can't effectively hold members of staff to account if they are unclear about what they have been employed to do.

If staff do not understand their roles and the expectations for practice, performance management activities will add little value.

Understanding performance management

Performance management is the term used to describe the activities and processes that we put in place to help staff meet our setting's WHY, HOW and WHAT. The purpose of those activities is to review the personal effectiveness of individual staff members, and to ensure that they continue to maintain the standards that we have set.

Highly effective performance management systems ensure that staff are:

- Provided with regular feedback about their performance,
- Supported to meet the standards and expectations set for practice,
- Enabled to grow knowledge, skills and talents so that they can continue to improve what they do and the services they provide.
(CIPD, 2018.)

This is also a way of ensuring that staff make connections between their work and the setting's purpose. There are four key components to an effective performance management system:

- **evidence gathering**
- **formal feedback**
- **informal feedback**
- **support**.
(Adapted from the definition used by Berkeley University)

Let's look at each of those components in more detail.

1. – Evidence gathering

If we are to truly understand the contribution that individual staff members make to our organisation's WHY, HOW and WHAT, we need a rounded view of their practice. Only when we have a broad range of information about our staff members will we gain an understanding of their strengths, weaknesses and where there are opportunities for staff to develop specialist knowledge and skills.

This range of information is likely to include:

- what staff know, understand and can do,
- what staff members do well, where they excel or show specific aptitude,
- where practice needs to develop,
- their ability to communicate, both verbally and in written form,
- how effective the staff member is at building relationships with children, parents and other team members,
- their disposition, attitude and behaviour.

Where might we see these elements?

It is likely that the vast majority of our current knowledge of staff comes from observations of practice, the way the environment has been structured, the quality and accuracy of children's files and the way in which they respond to requests or directions from their team leader, but other sources of information could come from:

Staff meetings or in-house training - Do we use these events to reflect on what practitioners know or don't know? Do they make significant contributions to discussions that help the meeting to move forward? Does their behaviour or attitude stand out during those events either for good or bad reasons?

The way the staff member raise concerns – There are any number of situations that this could apply to; raising a child protection concern (the way information has been recorded and/or presented), speaking up about something that isn't working well, a problem with a parent or even another member of staff. In all of these scenarios, we could gain knowledge about staff's skills and abilities, and their knowledge of our policies and procedures.

Scrutiny of written work – The EYFS is clear that all staff need have a good standard of written English, but is this something we routinely look for when we are reviewing children's records or sampling summative reports? Does written language in the environment provide children will good models of literacy?

Personal contributions to audits – It is common practice for settings to use audits such as the Early Childhood Environmental Rating Scales (ECERS) and the Infant and Toddler Environmental Rating Scales (ITERS) to assess practice, but do we use the knowledge we have gained from these events to provide individual staff members with feedback, to recognise their contribution, or to raise concerns about poor practice?

We may also want to consider how we include:

- Feedback from other members of staff, parents and professionals working with our setting,
- Inspections or external quality assurance visits that directly mention the work of individual members of staff or the work of a team,
- Thank you cards and presents, demonstrating that staff have gone above and beyond in the eyes of a parent,
- The approach taken to managing difficult parents,
- The way in which a staff member has supported and managed the behaviour of children who are finding nursery a challenge,
- Creative and inspiring environments that meet the needs and interests of the children.

Many of the activities above will form part of our current monitoring activities, however, in some settings, monitoring sits separately to performance management which means that there will be missed opportunities to use the examples above to gain a better understanding of our staff, and to recognise their contribution.

2. – Formal feedback

There are many names used to describe performance discussions: appraisals, supervisions, 1:1s, personal review meetings, etc., all of which refer to the face-to-face conversations that we have with a staff member about their performance.

The term that seems to be used frequently in settings is appraisal, the definition of which is:

"An act of assessing something or someone." The Oxford English dictionary (2018).

"The act of examining someone or something in order to judge their qualities, success, or needs" The Cambridge English dictionary (2018).

This seems like a good place to start, as it forces us to think about what we should be judging or assessing.

1:1 conversations provide opportunities to discuss the things that have an impact on performance. Typically, this will cover general health and well-being, things that may affect an individual's suitability to work with children, changes in personal circumstances, things that have gone well, and things that the staff member finds challenging. It will also include the manager's assessment of what is going well and where there may be room for improvement, the identification of performance targets to support the staff member to continue to grow both in confidence and competence, and professional development opportunities.

Many of these elements appear in the EYFS:
"3.11. Providers must tell staff that they are expected to disclose any convictions, cautions, court orders, reprimands and warnings that may affect their suitability to work with children (whether received before or during their employment at the setting)."

"3.19. Practitioners must not be under the influence of alcohol or any other substance which may affect their ability to care for children. If practitioners are taking medication which may affect their ability to care for children, those practitioners should seek medical advice. Providers must ensure that those practitioners only work directly with children if medical advice confirms that the medication is unlikely to impair that staff member's ability to look after children properly.

3.20. The daily experience of children in early years settings and the overall quality of provision depends on all practitioners having appropriate qualifications, training, skills and knowledge and a clear understanding of their roles and responsibilities. Providers must ensure that all staff receive induction training to help them understand their roles and responsibilities…Providers must support staff to undertake appropriate training and professional development opportunities to ensure they offer quality learning and development experiences for children that continually improves.

3.21. Providers must put appropriate arrangements in place for the supervision of staff who have contact with children and families. Effective supervision provides support, coaching and training for the practitioner and promotes the interests of children. Supervision should foster a culture of mutual support, teamwork and continuous improvement, which encourages the confidential discussion of sensitive issues.

3.22. Supervision should provide opportunities for staff to:

- discuss any issues – particularly concerning children's development or wellbeing, including child protection concerns
- identify solutions to address issues as they arise
- receive coaching to improve their personal effectiveness."
(EYFS, Pg. 21, 2018.)

We do, however, need to remember that the EYFS sets the minimum requirements for practice, therefore, the range of activities needed for performance management to be effective are not presented in any depth within the statutory framework. For example, the EYFS does not include the need for staff members to have performance targets, but it is implied.

This reinforces the need for us to have a good understanding of performance management. We need to be able to unpick what has been written in the statutory guidance and turn those statements into systems, processes and practice that will improve the knowledge and skills of our staff team, as well as improving the opportunities and experiences that we offer to children.

3. – Informal feedback

This often takes the form of a quick chat or impromptu discussion - the types of conversations that happen frequently throughout the day. It may be that we just popped in to share something, or to pass on a message and then end up having a conversation about practice. Maybe we are undertaking our usual 'walking the floor' activities to get a sense of how things are going when a member asked for advice or guidance.

These usually unscheduled interactions with staff help to keep us connected with what's happening, any issues or concerns, and how staff are coping and feeling. Keeping brief personal notes of significant interactions with staff will mean that we can remind ourselves of important points that were raised in between 1:1 discussions.

These notes do not need to record every interaction. We only need record things we wouldn't want to forget, such as when we've provided direction or guidance, things that have gone well or when we have had to 'nudge' staff to carry out specific tasks etc. Those bullet points or quick notes will not only act as a valuable aide-memoire, but will help to ensure that we demonstrate consistency in the way we manage our team.

4 - Support

Support is the last cornerstone of performance management. If we want to ensure that both our staff and our setting continue to move forward, we need to make a commitment to supporting the development of staff.

Support needs to be tailored to each individual's professional needs, in line with the needs of the organisation. This can be achieved through a wide range of mediums: training, coaching, mentoring, shadowing, being assigned specific tasks or temporary responsibilities, action research, reading, qualifications etc.

Through these different types of support, we will ensure that:
- staff remain able to fulfil their roles and responsibilities,
- staff develop a deeper level of knowledge and enhanced skills that will add value to what we do and how we do it,
- staff contribute to developing the setting's priorities and, where appropriate, strengthening leadership capacity.

When all these components are in place and implemented with consistency throughout the year, each staff member will be in the best possible position to meet the needs of their key children and of our organisation.

Managing your workload

The consistency of performance management activities is key. The job of a manager is a busy one; the role is far more complex than just monitoring what we do and managing people, so it is easy to become overloaded if our workload is not balanced. We, therefore, need to take a hard look at our responsibilities and, in particular, our span of control.

The term 'span of control' refers to the number of people that we directly line-manage. Countless articles offer a suggested **maximum** number of people to manage, which hovers between 6 and 8, but it would make more sense to base our span of control on our day-to-day workload. If we do not work directly with children, we should (in theory) have more capacity to manage staff than a manager who is also a key adult to a group of children. In many settings, managing staff has a huge impact on workload, often because leaders and managers are supervising too many people, even though there are others within the leadership team who could share some of this responsibility.

There may be reasons why managers are reticent to delegate leadership roles (loss of control and/or power, trust, staff are already burdened etc.), but being overloaded with people to manage will cause problems if the situation continues over an extended period of time.

Our interactions with staff and the support that we are able to provide are critical to the success of our setting. It is far better to be responsible for managing fewer people and to do this effectively, than trying to handle the 1:1 discussions of all staff and then not have the time, space or energy to make authentic connections with everyone. If we haven't got the time or capacity to ensure that our four key components are firmly embedded, we will not have the means to move practice forward at a reasonable pace. But there are even greater risks than a heavy workload. If staff are not being efficiently supported through a range of performance management activities, any of the following could happen:

- We may overlook underperforming staff,
- Staff may not feel valued because their contribution is not being recognised,
- Staff stop asking for advice and support because we are too busy,
- Staff may leave because they do not feel that their professional development needs are being met or supported,
- Our understanding of what is working well or what needs improvement becomes out of date quickly, and we could go on!

It is, therefore, worthwhile upskilling others within our senior leadership team to develop the confidence and abilities required to manage staff.

Managing your workload - span of control

Should you decide to review your span of control, you will need to think about your organisational structure and a pragmatic staffing hierarchy – in other words, who is best reporting to who. For example, if your management structure currently looks like this:

You may want to share the management of staff with your deputy, which could change your structure to look something like this:

You would still retain responsibility for the line management of the deputy and two other members of staff, but the deputy would now manage 3 members of staff (or less if you have concerns about your deputy's workload). This would reduce your immediate span of control to 3 members of staff rather than 6, and the 1:1 discussions with your deputy would be where you have conversations about the performance of the staff members that he/she manages.

In larger organisations, you may wish to distribute management responsibilities to more of your senior leadership team.

In doing this, the manager takes the responsibility for senior members of staff, and senior members of staff manage the practitioners they spend the most time working with.

If you work in a small setting, it is highly likely that the manager and deputy wear many hats, therefore, there is no point in using supporting statements. We can, however, ensure that the rest of the team are involved in performance management activities through peer-on-peer assessments. More on peer-on-peer will follow in this chapter.

The template, opposite, provides a format for capturing supporting statements. The dotted line is there to remind us that it would not be appropriate for other staff members to read the statements made by their colleagues.

Slips would only be completed if the member of staff felt that their contribution would add value to a performance discussion. If they have not worked with the staff member that term, or have had limited interactions, there would be little value in drafting a supporting statement.

I personally favour written supporting statements, as there is less room for misinterpretation. Experience would tell me that people are far more careful about the way they phrase feedback when they are asked to commit their views to paper!

After considering a more evenly distributed management structure, we can now turn our attention to the different types of evidence that will provide us with a rounded view of performance.

Playing to the strengths of our team

As managers, we are not always able to witness first-hand what staff do well and where support may be needed, so we need to develop a culture and systems that enable everyone to contribute to performance management activities.

Leadership roles

Staff members who hold specific responsibilities, such as the SENDCo, the Designated Safeguarding Lead, Health & Safety Officer etc, will be far better placed to make an assessment about what the staff know, understand and can do in relation to those areas of practice, therefore, it would make sense for anyone with a management or leadership role (where appropriate) to support our evidence gathering process.

This can be done either verbally (with the manager making notes), or by requesting that senior leaders provide a supporting statement. Written statements only need be brief and should convey information that either recognises the work of the practitioner or that is going to help them to develop their knowledge and skills further.

This way of working isn't something that should be entered into lightly. We will need to ensure that any staff member contributing to performance management records has had appropriate preparation or training to do so - anyone committing feedback to paper should understand what to document, and why. As a rule of thumb, statements need to be factual and support the development of practice, however, staff members must also be aware that their feedback could be used in disciplinary proceedings – hence the necessity for training!

The beauty of using supporting statements is that they create opportunities for meaningful discussion, rather than feeling like we're working through a checklist of points from the EYFS.

"If you are persistent, you'll get it. If you are consistent, you'll keep it up."
Harvey MacKay, Business guru and best-selling author

Supporting Statements Template

Supporting statement for: Debbie

Name: Victoria B   **Role: SENDCo**   **Date: 21/06/2019**

Work undertaken: I have had the opportunity to work closely with Debbie over the last 2-3 months.

Is there anything you would like to share about the work undertaken by this staff member?	Debbie met with T's parents to raise concerns about his behaviour this week. She demonstrated sensitivity and genuine care and concern. As a direct result, Mum shared how difficult she was finding things at home. This is a real breakthrough for partnership working with this family.
Do you have any recommendations for training and/or development?	None at this time.

Supporting statement for: Debbie

Name: Rosanne D   **Role: Safeguarding Lead**   **Date: 14/06/2019**

Work undertaken: I had the opportunity to work closely with Debbie last month.

Is there anything you would like to share about the work undertaken by this staff member?	In our last round of staff audits, Debbie struggled with the difference between Prevent and British values. This is something that we have had a conversation about.
Do you have any recommendations for training and/or development?	I have given Debbie a book on British values and we will have a chat about the implications for practice, once she has read it.

Supporting statement for: Debbie

Name: Mary S   **Role: Deputy & Room Leader**   **Date: 13/06/2019**

Work undertaken: Debbie and I work in the same room. I am the room supervisor.

Is there anything you would like to share about the work undertaken by this staff member?	Debbie has managed T's behaviour well over the past few weeks. She has used strategies effectively to redirect and distract T on a number of occasions. They have a good relationship and Debbie seems to be the only member of staff that T trusts at this time.
Do you have any recommendations for training and/or development?	None at this time.

If you find that supporting statements work well within your team, you may want to introduce something similar for staff members. You could use supporting statements to recognise the good work of others or to provide positive feedback. Staff members should not use them to provide development points or to raise concerns.

Peer-on-peer observation and assessment

With our senior leaders contributing to the picture we are gathering of individual members of staff, we obtain a more rounded view of what our team knows, understands and can do - but is that enough? Are there any other people that could contribute to our developing picture?

In Chapter 2 we talked about confirmation bias, and how it is preferable to have multiple views to ensure that we take in and act on all the evidence available to us. Whether we are a manager working in a small or large setting, in ratio with children or not included in ratios, the likelihood is that we will have limited opportunities to formally observe practice. It, therefore, makes sense to widen our understanding of staff's performance by introducing peer-on-peer assessment.

Peer-on-peer assessment is an incredibly powerful tool, because it involves everyone in continuous improvement. When implemented rigorously, it creates a learning community where staff welcome feedback from their colleagues because they know that it will be constructive and help them to grow. In these settings, professional challenge is welcome and there are healthy (and sometimes heated) debates about practice, because everyone wants to be the best they can be for the benefit of the children.

If you know little about peer-on-peer assessment, here is a quick overview of what it entails:

1. It provides each staff member with a view of practice from the perspective of colleagues who work alongside them. It involves practitioners observing each other's practice and providing feedback about what worked well, and where they believe practice could be further developed.
2. It requires the observer to observe what is happening and then make a judgement about what they have seen and heard (using the same skills we already adopt in the process of observing children). This results in judgements being made about what the practitioner knows, understands and does well, as well as identifying opportunities to improve practice, knowledge and skills.
3. It is (or should be) a two-way learning process. Even though one person is observing the practice of another, the process enables both parties to learn more about

themselves, their strengths and potential areas for development. When the process is structured well, feedback provides chances for the observer to also share things that they have learned, or that they found useful for their own practice.

Creating the right environment for peer-on-peer assessment

Every practitioner will have elements of their practice that are good and elements that could be developed further. The problem is that the thought of a colleague (and possibly a friend) observing our practice leaves many feeling anxious, nervous or uncomfortable. So, how can we create an environment that enables staff members to feel less apprehensive about peer-on-peer observation?

It has been well documented in pure, social and organisational psychology that human beings, at all ages and stages of life, constantly seek the answer to two questions: 'Am I safe?' and 'Do I matter?'. In order for a practitioner to be more comfortable with the notion of 'peer-on-peer', they need to feel that they are working in a safe environment, that they trust their colleagues, and believe that those they work with value what they do and the contribution that they make.

In order to create sound foundations for peer-on-peer assessment, we need to examine the culture of our setting and in doing so, explore whether we can answer these two questions for all staff.

These types of questions will help:

- Do we work in an environment which encourages staff to test out new things, even knowing that they won't always work?
- Have we developed environments where practitioners have enough autonomy to use their initiative, and to find creative solutions to problems?
- Do staff members feel safe to admit when they have got something wrong or when things aren't going well?
- Do we see staff members asking each other for help and support?
- Have we created environments where we can have honest discussions about things that have gone wrong, without casting blame?
- Do we regularly celebrate success, recognising the

work of individuals or of the team as a whole?

- Do staff consistently receive feedback about their performance?
- Does the process of feedback recognise individual strengths, identify areas that will make a difference to professional growth, and do we then commit to putting things in place to address those areas?
- Have we provided enough opportunities for staff to get to know each other well?
- Do staff demonstrate respectful relationships in front of children and when they are alone with work colleagues?
- Do staff show trust in each other?
- Have we made assumptions about those two questions or do we have hard evidence that staff feel safe and that their contribution is valued?

As always, it is beneficial for us to think about the evidence we have in order to support our answer(s). If we cannot answer those questions for all staff, this may indicate that we do not know staff as well as we first thought. The harsh reality is that if we have not adequately established firm foundations for peer-on-peer, its implementation is likely to result in a bunch of people going through a process because 'the boss' said they needed to. It will add little, if any value, to what we do and, in extreme cases, it could antagonise poor working relationships.

Andy Cope who is a renowned speaker on the topic of motivation and positive psychology, writes and speaks regularly on various leadership topics, but from all the things that I've read and seen, this resonated with me the most; Andy believes that if staff feel safe and their contribution is valued, most of our team will be happy. Happy people tend to be ill less frequently (or make the effort to still come in when they are feeling a bit poorly). They trust their colleagues, they are more likely to work well as part of a team and are more inclined to support each other. But most importantly, they tend to have a greater level of positivity and motivation when at work, which shines through when they are with children.

The alternative is people who take lots of sick days, staff members who are constantly negative, individuals who choose not to use their initiative, and there will be some practitioners that are literally getting their coats on as the last child is leaving the building because they can't wait to clock-off.
(Cope, 2018.)

It is therefore clear that, if we are able to create a culture in which staff feel both safe and valued, a peer-on-peer approach will be far more effective.

Next is the importance of **ownership**.

If you intend to implement peer-on-peer assessment (or are using it already), have you thought about how you intend staff to feel connected to the process and to see a value in it?

Developing a criteria for peer-on-peer together is hugely rewarding. We've already established that being part of the development of something helps to deepen our understanding of it. In the case of peer-on-peer, being able to contribute to the design of the criteria that is going to be used to assess one's own practice can reduce the fear and anxiety of someone 'judging' what we do. It will also help to establish a value to the activity, because staff are identifying the things that they feel are important.

I recently worked with a setting who wanted to refresh their approach to peer-on-peer. Historically, they had used criteria that had been constructed by the management team and although peer-on-peer assessments were happening, the staff were neither comfortable nor confident with the process itself. At the point at which I got involved, the majority of staff felt that peer-on-peer was just something that needed to be done, so they got on and did it without passion, commitment or a sense of why they were doing it.

The consistency of approach was variable across the team due to different interpretations of the criteria, and no-one really saw a value in it because individuals were so anxious about providing feedback to their colleagues (and friends), that everything they shared was positive.

The leadership team decided that the only way to improve this situation was to scrap everything that had previously existed and to develop something from scratch which would involve the whole team. The hope was that working together would mean that everyone was part of the discussion about the development of the criteria, the team would identify elements of practice that made a difference to children, and that going through the process together would help everyone to understand what the observer would be looking at and why.

The benefits gained from just one 2.5 hour staff meeting dedicated to peer-on-peer assessment were:

- Everyone had a voice and was heard - Activities were planned so that everyone had the opportunity to share their thoughts and ideas.
- Everyone was involved in the design of the observational criteria – The discussions that took place were far more in-depth than the management team had anticipated because staff self-selected to focus on what they needed to do to meet children's needs.
- They identified key points in their session and week to carry out peer observations – Conversations again

exceeded the expectations of the management team because when we turned our attention to conducting observations, staff wanted to ensure that practice was observed at key times, which would help them to understand what was working well and where practice could be developed further (rather than their previous system of 'I need to observe you, I can do it today at 10.45am. Is that ok with you?').
- Working out the process together gave everyone more confidence to be an observer and to be observed.

I certainly don't want to give the impression that one development session on peer-on-peer will magically solve any problems associated with its implementation! However, laying the foundations together as a team meant that staff appreciated both its purpose and value, that they had a detailed understanding of the criteria, and of what it meant for practice (which would address the previous issues of consistency). This gave all staff a greater level of confidence and competence when carrying out observations.

If you decide to develop your peer-on-peer criteria with staff, you will need to ensure that statements are clear and that the criteria do not include statements that could mean different things to different members of staff. Do not allow criteria such as:

- Use of body language
- Using language appropriate for the age of the child
- How practitioners deal with children's behaviour
- The modelling of language.

You need to unpick each of these statements further so that observations can be carried out with consistency. For example, if the team feel that the use of body language is important, what is it that we need to look for? The more precise the criteria, the less chance there is of misinterpretation.

Formal discussions

We have focused on what makes a performance management system effective and will have put systems in place to gather evidence, however, what managers will often struggle with is the 1:1 discussions and, in particular, the sorts of question that we ought to ask. Managers often report that it's a difficult balancing act between addressing the points in the EYFS and having a meaningful conversation about practice which enables us to make genuine connections with staff, in the short time that they have.

To gain a rounded view of practice and the things that affect performance, we need to find opportunities to discuss:

- Health and well-being which would include changes in personal circumstances, general health and an understanding of each staff member's workload,
- What staff know, understand and can do so that we can identify where practice can be developed or enhanced,
- Where professional development could support the growth of knowledge, skills and talents,
- The effectiveness of safeguarding practices and any concerns about children, staff or practice within our setting,
- The progress of key children,
- Whether targets set in previous discussions have been achieved,
- What our setting does well and where there is room for improvement,
- Where staff members can contribute to the setting's priorities for improvement.

1:1 discussions

So, we're in a room, face-to-face with a member of staff; we know the topics that we need to cover...but we may be nervous, and our team member is most certainly going to be anxious too. What can we do to manage this situation to ensure that we get what we need from the conversation, and that our colleague is given the opportunity to share everything they would wish to?

Firstly, we need to prepare. Going into a face-to-face/1:1 discussion with a staff member unprepared is disrespectful and sends a clear message that we do not value what they do – even if that's not true! We, therefore, need to review the information that we have gathered previously, to understand what it is telling us before our meeting. We need the opportunity to think about the information that we want to gain from our conversation and the areas that need to be covered.

Having a set of prompts to refer to, can support our preparation. It will ensure that we cover all the things we need to and, with some careful writing, we can devise

open-ended questions that will encourage the staff member to share a greater level of detail. (This will help us to avoid one-word responses to questions).

Initially, using prompts may look like we're following a script, but as we become more familiar and confident with the process, we will find that we may only need to use bullet points or even keywords to jog our memory.

What follows, are examples of general prompts that you may find useful during face-to-face meetings with staff.

Questions that may help us to understand what staff know, understand and can do (personal effectiveness)

- How have things been going since we last met?
- What has gone really well for you? / What has been successful since we last met?
- Is there anything that you've found difficult or challenging?
- Have you found any solutions or is this still a difficulty/ challenge?
- How could I or other team members help you to overcome this difficulty/challenge?
- Where do you feel you need support to develop or improve aspects of your practice?
- What parts of your job have you enjoyed most (since we last met)?
- What parts of your job have you enjoyed least (since we last met)?
- What areas of practice interest you?
- What do you think your next set of professional development opportunities need to focus on? / Have you thought about developing your knowledge and skills further? What might your next steps be?

Questions that will help us to review children's progress

- Which of your key children are you most concerned about and why?
- What is currently in place for Alice? What are you doing differently to help her make more progress?
- How much do parents know about your concerns? What has been shared?
- What are your future plans for Alice? / What do you think needs to happen next? / When will this be in place?
- Are you being supported by the SENDCo/ Safeguarding Lead? What plans have you made together to support Alice?

- Which children are working within their developmental milestones? / Have they made much progress?
- What are you doing to make sure that activities and opportunities offer enough challenge for all of your key children?
- How do you know that you are providing enough challenge? What evidence do you have?
- Are there any children who are exceeding their developmental milestones? If so, what are you doing to make sure that there is an appropriate level of challenge for them?
- Are those children exceeding in all areas? If not, what are you doing to help them make more progress in these areas?
- Is there anything you feel you need support with?
- Are you confident that you can meet the needs of all your key children or are there areas where you feel you need more knowledge/support?

Questions that will help us to focus on professional development

- What training or development opportunities have you been able to access since we last met?
- What impact has that had on your practice? /What difference has it made to you and/or your practice?
- Do you think I'd see a difference in your interactions with children/your approach to safeguarding/ your environment/the way you observe, assess and plan for children? (As appropriate to the conversation) What might those differences be?

- Is there anything that you could share with staff about this event?
- If there is something that can be shared with staff, how would you like to disseminate this information? (Team meeting, writing up your experience etc.)
- We've talked about things that have gone well and things that could be developed further, so what do you think your next development priorities should focus on?

Questions that will help us to understand safeguarding concerns

- Do you have any safeguarding concerns about your key children?
- How are relationships with his/her parents/carers/ family?
- How is Alice getting on during her sessions?
- Are there any changes in her behaviour?
- What have you already put in place?
- Is there anything else that we could be doing for her?
- Do you have any safeguarding worries?
- Are you unsure whether something may be a safeguarding concern?
- Do you have any concerns about our setting or our practice?
- Do you have any safeguarding concerns about the conduct of staff?
- Are there any areas of safeguarding where you feel less confident?
- If there are, what do you think your next steps ought to be?

Questions that will help us to focus on the needs of our setting

- What do you feel that we do really well as a setting? (Response) Why do you think that is?
- What do you feel that staff do really well? (Response) Why do you think that is?
- What do you think we could do better? (Response) Why do you think that is?
- Do you have any thoughts on how we could improve…?
- Do you know what our key priorities for improvement are at the moment?
- What do you feel that you could do to help us address these priorities?

Source: Performance Management Templates, pg.5-7. Early Years Fundamentals Ltd, 2018.

THINK ABOUT...

Top tips

To use all of those questions would take a considerable amount of time, so we need to identify what is important to ask during a face-to-face meeting and to identify the questions that may be covered by other activities, such as, room meetings where we discuss, for example, the progress of individual children and review the quality of observations and assessment. Not everything has to be done through a 1:1 discussion.

Do not fill silence!

Just as we do with children, we need to give staff time to process the questions we have asked and to formulate a response. So, if you are tempted to jump in or feel that there is an awkward silence, hang in there. Leaving a gap of around 5 seconds is usually long enough to prompt staff to speak up.

If we truly want to make the most of our 1:1 discussions with staff, we can also provide a set of prompts for them to consider prior to our meeting. This will give each staff member a chance to gather their own thoughts and to reflect on practice. You may, therefore, want to circulate some of the general points above to staff a few days before their scheduled 1:1 discussion.

All of these general prompts imply that things are going relatively well. The questions give a feeling that our conversations would focus on development and growth rather than concerns about practice, but what if things are not going well and we need to share concerns about practice or conduct?

Raising concerns

Here are several strategies that may help you to have an honest and open conversation with staff when practice isn't where you need it to be. This could be during 1:1 discussions or you may feel the need to have a specific meeting, if you need to act quickly.

Focus on the specific area of practice and ask your colleague to talk about the things that are going well, and where there are challenges.

- How do you feel (refer to the activity or piece of work) it went?
- Which parts do you feel went really well?
- Which parts would you do differently and why?

Agree with the statements you know to be true and provide your view of why aspects of practice were successful, using phrases such as...'I think (refer to success) went really well because' or 'the parts that I thought worked well were...'.

Then refer back to the answer that the staff member gave when talking about what they would do differently and why. If what has been said matches the concerns that you wished to raise, you can focus on solutions, but if there is a difference you must take this opportunity to raise your concerns.

Wherever possible, use observations or provide examples of what happened/what was said so that you can help the member of staff view things from your perspective.

Beware the feedback sandwich!

In the past, it was thought that it was better or kinder to give feedback as a sandwich – some positive comments before raising concerns and then some positive comments toward the end of the discussion to finish on a high. However, behaviour psychology tells us that our instinct is to latch onto information that we feel is negative, particularly when it concerns us, so if we deliver positive comments at the beginning of our conversation and some towards the end, the likelihood is that the last set of positives will be lost. The staff member is unlikely to be able to take in any of the positive comments after hearing something that they perceived to be 'bad' because they will be focused on what they did, whether they agree or not with the comments and the course of action the manager is proposing. Therefore, the new rule is, positive comments first and concerns last.

Finally, ask your colleague what they think would be the best course of action to resolve the situation, or gain their view of what might help them move their practice forward. You may not always agree, but it is a starting point; it opens a discussion about moving forward and it will help you to see things from their perspective.

The key question we need to ask ourselves is, 'is this an issue of underperformance?'

Managing underperformance

Underperformance is likely to conjure up images of staff members who are terrible at their job, those who cause trouble amongst colleagues or are constantly negative. You may have individuals in mind who do the absolute minimum and walk out of the door the moment they can - regardless of how prepared the setting is for the following day. Whatever thoughts came to mind, the term has negative connotations and no-one would like to think of themselves as underperforming. There are, however, periods of time when staff members may find it difficult to meet the standards or expectations that we have set for practice, and this could be for any number of reasons. For example:

- A member of staff who has returned from a long period of sickness,
- A member of staff who has taken time out to look after their family,
- A member of staff has just been employed or taken on a new role within the setting,
- A member of staff is experiencing stressful/emotional events in their home/personal life,
- An individual finds it hard to develop the knowledge and skills required to perform their job properly,
- An individual is not able to meet the standards set, due to their attitude, behaviour or poor decision making,
- We haven't trained staff well enough to perform their duties to expectation,
- We haven't been clear about their roles, responsibilities and the expectations for practice.

This list typically falls into 3 categories:

- Capability
- Conduct
- Poor leadership and management.

Capability (the staff member currently lacks the ability to perform to the standards required)

Capability has two strands; the first is that the staff member does not have the ability to fulfil all aspects of their role due to illness (or ill-health) and the second is due to a lack of knowledge, skills or aptitude. Grounds of illness or ill-health are likely to be covered by a sickness policy, whilst the lack of skills, knowledge and aptitude will be covered by a capability policy.

Examples of capability issues

Sickness/Ill-health Policy
Examples
■ Illness
■ A long-term medical condition
■ Mental-health
■ Personal trauma and/or bereavement
■ Overloaded/overwhelmed
■ Loss of control

Capability Policy
Examples
■ Gaps in knowledge or skills
■ Not able to meet the standards/expectations set for practice
■ Lack of confidence
■ New to role
■ Returning after a long absence and needs to 'catch-up'
■ Tries hard but doesn't seem to adapt to changes easily

Conduct (the behaviour and/or attitude of the staff member)

The key difference between conduct and capability is that in issues of capability, the staff member is unlikely to have chosen to be in this situation, and most people want to improve or move practice/the situation forward, whereas in issues relating to conduct, individuals are likely to have made a deliberate choice to act or behave in a certain way.

The examples below will help to clarify this further.

Examples

- Does the minimum
- No pride in their work, so standards are low
- Obstructive, constantly negative
- Undermines leadership
- Doesn't take instruction
- Unwilling to help others
- Rude or aggressive towards staff
- Rude or aggressive towards parents
- Inappropriate use of social media
- Poor time management
- Inappropriate behaviour in or outside of work
- Fraud
- Absent without consent
- Significant breach of policy
  (CIPD, 2018)

Poor leadership and management

There will be many clear-cut scenarios which can be identified as either a capability or conduct issue, but we also need to consider the role that we may have played in each scenario. Have we provided enough training? Have we been clear about our expectations and ensured that each staff member understands what is required of them? Have we been meeting with staff frequently enough to provide feedback on their performance?

Let's take a couple of examples that will help to put this into context.

Scenario 1.

It is rare to take on a new member of staff or for a staff member to step up into a new role and for them to have absolutely everything that we're looking for. For example, there could be gaps in their knowledge, they still need further training, or they may still lack experience in some areas of practice. None of this is a problem, provided that we put the appropriate support, training and mentoring in place to address those gaps.

Scenario 2.

If we take up a management or leadership post in an established team, we have no idea at the start what members of staff know, understand and can do, so it falls on us to gather evidence that will give us a more rounded picture of practice.

If the emerging picture is that we identify weak areas of practice or there are inconsistencies, we will need to take swift action to address those issues which we have identified.

In both cases, the members of staff will continue to underperform until we put the appropriate support in place, and if we don't, we are failing in our management duties.

How to record our discussions

We have established what we want to ask and also identified ways to broach concerns about practice, but the conversation alone is not enough. What we record, and how, is a crucial part of the process.

It is easy to find examples of 1:1 discussion templates and there is no problem with adopting models from colleagues or the internet, as long as we are clear about what we need to record and why. If you already have a template in place, it may be worth comparing its headings against the following:

Key areas for 1:1 discussions

Headings	Reason
Name of the staff member	To identify the member of staff
Name of the manager	To identify the current manager (or to be able to identify previous managers, should this ever be needed).
Date	To provide an accurate record of when the discussion happened and to show the frequency of discussions when several 1:1 discussions are brought together.
Date of next meeting	Committing to a future date is helpful to ensure that meetings happen with consistency and frequency.
A review of the previous targets set	To ensure that the staff member has completed all previous targets set to a satisfactory standard.
Salient points discussed	To record brief notes of the conversation held with the staff member, which should include the manager's feedback, responses from staff, any issues or concerns shared by the staff member and events or training accessed. Our notes will provide evidence of what was discussed, so that when reflecting back on previous notes, we should be able to identify the progress being made by each staff member or have evidence of the lack of progress. Our notes should not provide a verbatim account of who said what; we just need to record the important points raised by both parties, unless we feel that a quote adds important information.
New/amended targets	To provide direction, address issues of underperformance and to support professional growth.
Agreed date for completion	To ensure that the target/area of work is not on-going for an extended period of time.
Any actions for the manager	To identify any support needed from the manager or other members of staff.
Training/professional development opportunities	To enhance knowledge, skills and talents and support the development of weaker areas of practice, or to develop the knowledge/expertise within the setting.
Signature of the manager and the staff member	To confirm that both parties agree to the content of the record and that the notes taken were an accurate representation of the discussion.
Date next to signatures	To indicate how close to the actual discussion the notes were signed and agreed.

These key areas do not necessarily need to appear as specific boxes on our template but should appear somewhere in our discussion notes. For your convenience, a template has been placed at Annex F. This is a format I regularly use when delivering training on performance management.

How often do you hold 1:1 conversations?

Each member of staff should have a formal 1:1 discussion regularly across the year, (usually this is 3 or 4 times a year depending on whether you work in terms or in quarters). However, if they are too close together, we run the risk of not giving staff enough time to implement the target or targets that were set during the last discussion, and if we hold meetings too far apart, we risk not being able to spot or deal swiftly with issues of underperformance.

Regular meetings will provide opportunities to share how things are going (from the perspective of the staff member and the manager), to receive words of encouragement and recognition when things have gone well, which will help staff to stay motivated and to know that their contribution is valued.

Regular interactions, (both formal and informal) will ensure that we have an honest and on-going dialogue about performance.

Frequently occurring issues in Ofsted inspections

Monitoring and managing performance is a key issue, that appear with consistency in 'inadequate' and 'requires improvement' inspection outcomes.

In the academic year September 2017- July 2018 these actions and recommendations were commonly found in inspection reports:

"Management of Staff

- Implement effective supervision arrangements that provide staff with support, coaching and training to raise the quality of teaching and learning.
- Refine staff supervision sessions to effectively identify and address weaknesses in staff practice ensuring that teaching is at a consistently good level.
- Develop staffs on-going opportunities to access professional development and evaluate the impact of those experiences.
- Ensure that staff are clear about their roles, responsibilities and the expectations for practice.
- Ensure that supervision happens regularly and consistently for all members of staff.
- Ensure that effective supervision and monitoring arrangements accurately identify and quickly address weaker areas of practice and teaching."

Sources: Inspection Trends: A Report for the Early Years Private, Voluntary & Independent Sector, Early Years Fundamentals, 2018.

All of the Ofsted actions and recommendations above have been addressed thoroughly in this chapter, but you may wish to use the statements to create an audit to evaluate your current systems and practice.

Chapter 4: Accurate self-evaluation and action planning

If we have followed the processes outlined in the previous chapters, we will now have a rigorous monitoring framework and an on-going cycle of performance management activities. The question now is how do we use all that information to give us a rounded picture of our strengths, areas for development, risks to our business and immediate priorities?

In isolation, individual monitoring activities and performance reviews will give us small pieces of our quality assurance jigsaw. Each individual piece is important, however, it will only ever give us a limited view of practice and performance.

In order for us to see the whole picture, we need to bring all of our jigsaw pieces together to understand what is working well and what isn't; what needs our attention and, more importantly, to identify any issues that are of critical importance to our business.

Without a full picture or a broad overview, we will be unable to manage risks both effectively and in a timely manner, and there is also a possibility that we might invest time in things that should be much further down our 'to do' list.

In highly effective settings, the outcomes of monitoring activities are either added to one central document as they go along or brought together at several points in the year. In both cases, the management team will review the totality of their information and data to gain a comprehensive view of the overall quality of the provision, 2-3 times a year.

Why isn't this just an annual event?

Different aspects of our data are likely to change throughout the year as we work to improve areas of practice, or because we may suddenly find an element of practice that is no longer working well.

Without regular reviews of our monitoring data, what we define to be our strengths and areas for development can quickly become out of date and our priorities for improvement may not necessarily be addressing our most pressing issues. We, therefore, need a systematic way of recording and summarising what our monitoring and performance management activities are telling us, to keep accurate and up-to-date information that will support the decision-making process about immediate and future priorities.

Analysing monitoring data

We have a clear view of what we need to monitor, and have identified criteria which will give us a precise understanding of what we need to look at and for; what we need to address now is how our criteria will provide us with information that will help us to decide where our strengths and areas for development lie.

In order for us to be able to draw accurate conclusions from our data, we need to decide how we are going to measure our criteria. We need to decide on a format that can be used consistently to build up a picture over time which will help us to understand, for example, if

the standards and expectations that we set for practice have been embedded, if the quality of our provision is being sustained or whether our children are making better progress because of changes we have made.

Regardless of whether we're measuring quantity (how many times something happened or how often), or writing about what we have observed, we need to design a format that will make it as easy as possible to extract key information, such as what is working well, what isn't, what could or needs to be improved, and any recommendations the reviewer/observer would like to make about how to take practice forward.

A good example of this would be an Ofsted report.

Example of an Ofsted report

A Cottage in the Woods
Community Interest Company,
Wiggleton Community Hall,
Wiggleton,
Derbyshire, DE12 3AB

Inspection Date:		03/09/2018
Previous Inspection:		Not applicable
The quality and standard of the early years provision	**This inspection:**	**Requires improvement 3**
	Previous inspection:	**Not applicable**
Quality of education		**Requires improvement 3**
Behaviour and attitudes		**Requires improvement 3**
Personal development		**Requires improvement 3**
Leadership and management		**Requires improvement 3**

Summary of key findings for parents

This is a provision that requires improvement

- **The manager does not effectively check the quality of teaching to tackle weaknesses in practice swiftly. As a result, teaching is inconsistent.**
- **Staff do not consistently make effective use of information they gain from their observations of what children can do, to plan consistently for the next stage of development.**
- **Systems for monitoring the progress made by different groups of children are not sufficiently embedded.**

It has the following strengths

- **The provider, manager and staff demonstrate a commitment and willingness to continue to improve the quality of the nursery and outcomes for children.**
- **Staff develop effective partnerships with parents, other professionals and agencies. They agree strategies to help children who have special educational needs and/or disabilities make sufficient progress in their learning and development.**

I've designed this fictitious inspection narrative in the style of an Ofsted inspection report to illustrate my point. The first thing you'll notice is that the front page summarises all the important information, making it easy for the reader to understand the view of this mock Ofsted report.

From just one page, we understand that:

- This is the setting's first inspection.
- The setting's first major weakness is in leadership and management (as no-one in the management team is effectively reviewing the quality of teaching and learning and providing feedback to staff that then enables practitioners to develop their knowledge and understanding of observation, assessment and any next steps).
- The second major weakness is that the leadership team have not embedded their systems for monitoring the progress of children, so they will be unable to identify groups of children who perform less well than their peers etc.

Choosing formats that help us to extract key information quickly are of paramount importance as we don't want to add to our workload by creating systems that are labour intensive. Once you have devised your formats, think about adding a summary or quick overview table at the front of the report which will summarise the reviewer's key findings and recommendations. Evidence of how the reviewer came to their judgement is still important, but it can sit behind the summary, just as it does in an Ofsted report.

THINK ABOUT...

Just because we are talking about different formats of monitoring does not mean that you need to generate lots of different templates or huge amounts of reviews. Remain focused on the activities that you identified in your monitoring framework.

What to record

By now we probably have a good idea of the types of formats that we will use to capture our monitoring activities, but what we write is even more important if our data is to provide an accurate view of our strengths and areas for development.

Anyone who is carrying out monitoring activities needs to have a clear understanding of the difference between evaluative and descriptive language. If we (or members of our team) are just describing what we see and hear, monitoring activities will add little value to our knowledge of what's working well and what isn't. However, if staff use evaluative language, they will make judgements about the effectiveness of practice.

This is much easier to do when staff have criteria or a set of questions to work from. The clearer we are about what we need staff to look at and for and the information we want to gain, the more likely we are to receive the staff member's perception of what is happening and their assessment of why it is working well, or not. It is much harder for staff members to provide feedback about how well something is working if we don't provide guidance. It's easy to fall into the trap of just writing about what has been seen and heard, which is unlikely to deepen our knowledge of what we know about our setting.

The use of descriptive language is often a sticking point during inspections. I've read countless inspection reports which cite the need for the provider to clearly identify strengths and weaknesses and to demonstrate the impact of actions taken in self-evaluation.

The examples below should help to clarify the difference. An example of descriptive language:

- Children have access to the outdoor environment each day.
- Children are able to access resources independently within the environment.
- Each child has a learning journal which their key person will update, identifying what children know, understand and can do.

Each of the statements above is factual, but adds little value to what we know about what's working well and what isn't.

An example of evaluative language

- Performance management activities such as observations of practice, environmental audits and the scrutiny of planning and learning journals identified the need for the whole staff team to focus on the use of mathematical language.

- Maths training was delivered in March, and written feedback from staff showed an increase in mathematical knowledge and an increased understanding of where and how maths activities could be delivered within our environment.
- Observations of adult: child interactions now show 4 out of 5 staff members confidently using mathematical language and concepts.
- Observations of practice now show children independently using maths language in play.

In the second set of statements, we can see that judgements have been made about the quality of maths provision which has helped the leadership team to pinpoint an area of development. Plans were then made to address the issue and the writer has evaluated the impact of those activities. The language being used is clearly conveying to the reader that there was an issue, that the setting made plans to address it and that those plans had a positive impact on practice. The example of descriptive language is factual, whereas the example of evaluative language analyses what has happened to date, and the impact of the actions taken.

Interpreting your findings

Interpreting the findings from monitoring activities needs to happen at 2 levels, in order for the data to make a valid and accurate contribution to our overall view of the quality of our provision:

- analysis of the individual monitoring activity: what is working well, what isn't and where are the priorities for development?
- analysis of the overall picture by bringing together related monitoring activities. For example, looking at what our monitoring data is telling us about the quality of teaching and learning or how effective our safeguarding systems are. By bringing all of the data for a specific area of practice together, we should be able to identity our key strengths in this area as well as weaker areas of practice. We will then be able to make decisions about improvements and what should be addressed first.

But how do we capture all of this in a way which provides just enough detail to enable us to plan for the future, without creating a huge amount of paperwork?

Recording self-evaluation in a way that works for you

Self-evaluation enables us to see the big picture and it helps us to manage our own workload, and that of our team. By understanding our strengths and areas for development across the whole of our setting, we can prioritise the issues that pose the greatest risks to our business and park those that are less important!

The term self-evaluation, however, became synonymous with the Self Evaluation Form (SEF) which Ofsted published to help providers capture evidence of their monitoring activities. Many leaders and managers started to regard self-evaluation as something that needed to be developed for their inspection, rather than seeing it as a process that would enable them to manage business risk and to continue to improve the services offered to children and their families. Although the SEF had never been mandatory, huge numbers of providers used it because they felt that it would put them in a better position during an inspection.

In April 2018, Ofsted removed their self-evaluation template. This move was taken to provide settings with the same level of autonomy experienced by schools (as the Ofsted template for schools had long since been removed). Nevertheless, the withdrawal caused a great deal of concern in the early years sector.

Many providers felt conflicted; do they still use the SEF template, or do they do something different, and if they do opt to do something different, what do they replace the Ofsted template with? The greatest fear for providers was producing something that their inspector would not approve of, or value.

The Ofsted SEF is still a valid and useful document so there is no need to abandon it, if the format works for you. The quality and effectiveness of our self-evaluation document will be driven by the depth and breadth of our monitoring activities, so the template used to capture this information is largely irrelevant.

As long as we are able to summarise our strengths, areas of concern, priorities for improvement and the impact of any actions we've taken, it is of little consequence where the document comes from or who developed it.

Effective self-evaluation

For self-evaluation to be truly effective, we need to capture our setting's story/journey so far, which goes way beyond just identifying what is working well and what isn't.

Why? Looking at our monitoring information and data together will give us an understanding of what is happening now, but to gain a more accurate view of quality we need to be able to look at strands of our data over time. For example, what does the overall picture of teaching and learning look like now? What did it look like last term and the term before?

Comparing historical data in this way enables us to track our progress and to understand where we may have barriers, challenges or blocks. This does not have to be a massively complex piece of work, but it does require a disciplined approach to saving previous versions of our 'SEF'.

The ability to take a retrospective look at our data will also enable us to identify trends over a period time (in the same way we do with cohort tracking) and we can use our improvement journey to learn from previous mistakes or refer back to things that went well. Being able to look back at our journey so far is also a tremendous motivator as it enables us to see just how far our setting has come.

THINK ABOUT...

Saving your self-evaluation documents

When saving your self-evaluation documents, I recommend that you save each updated version with a slightly different name. I use this format '2019/01/01 SEF spring v1' and my updated version would look something like this '2019/04/01 SEF summer v1'. Putting the date first will ensure that when you come to search for the latest version of your 'SEF', all related documents will appear in date order making it easy to find the most recent version.

You may also wish to think about version control (which is the 'v' in the examples above and below). Version control enables us to store different versions of the same file so that we can look back on previous information/data or ensure that we are working on the most up-to-date document. If you have made small amendments/updates to a document you may want to save the document as, '2019/01/01 SEF spring v2' to indicate that the spring term document was amended and saved as version 2. This is particularly useful if there are several people who are likely to read and/or update your self-evaluation materials.

How long should I keep my SEF documents for?

Any self-evaluation material older than 3 years needs to be archived as it is likely to be too out of date to provide anything of significant value. Older documents should be archived in the short term and then deleted in line with your document disposal schedule.

Developing a self-evaluation framework

Devising one comprehensive central self-evaluation format or framework can be quite complex when we think about the breadth of our monitoring activities, so the following may act as a useful guide. If we wish to use a format that captures the journey of our setting as well as external factors that may influence self-evaluation, we need to capture these key areas:

- the changing demographics of the community(ies) that we serve (to understand our client base and their needs, which may change over time),
- significant changes that have affected our provision within the last 12 months (both good and bad),

- the views of other professionals, inclusive of previous inspection actions and recommendations to ensure that we sustain changes that have been made to comply with/address legislation or external recommendations,
- the things that are working well within our setting,
- the things that aren't working well,
- the things that need immediate attention,
- the actions we need to take, the actions we've taken and the impact or difference those actions have made (which can be presented as an action plan).

Our self-evaluation document needs to provide us with a way of summarising and communicating what our monitoring systems tell us about the quality and smooth running of our provision. We also need to bear in mind that as leaders and managers, Ofsted's judgement of effective leadership is made on the basis of the accuracy of our self-evaluation, the way in which we take swift and effective action to address weaknesses and our understanding of the impact or the difference that our actions have made.

Using demographics to our advantage

Understanding the communities that we serve, or our client base, isn't about ticking boxes for Ofsted. By understanding local demographics, we gain insight into levels of income, employment status, levels of education, ethnicity and age ranges within a given community. This can help us to make important decisions about our business, the way that we deliver services to our families and our ability to meet the needs of children. For example, our demographics could alert us to changes in our community make-up. What if there was a steady increase of Eastern European families? How would we know? How would we reach out to them so that they knew we were there? And do we have systems in place that would enable us to meet the needs of children whose primary language was not English? Demographics can also help us to understand some of the difficulties our families face. Local authority information may show, for example, high levels of crime, domestic abuse, social care involvement or low levels of education which may influence the services that we offer, the way we present information and the need to develop relationships with organisations that provide support for families. All of these factors will influence what we do with children and how we develop relationships with our parents.

In short, local demographics enable us to understand needs, barriers and challenges within our community. This will put us in a better position to support children, signpost families to appropriate services and to train our staff to respond appropriately to those needs.

THINK ABOUT...

From a business strategy point of view, demographics can also help us to plan for the future and reshape our services to meet community need. If we saw an increase in births locally, we may be able to make internal changes that enable us to take more babies and toddlers. What about the development of a new housing estate? Might that present an opportunity to widen our client base or might it be a threat because the plans also include a new primary school with early years places?

If you have never used local demographics before, your local authority is a good place to start. They profile individual electoral wards and some of the information held will even go down to street level. This information comes from a range of different sources, so some elements will be updated annually, whilst others may be less frequent. We can gain access to this information through our local authority's website or a 'Google search' for 'electoral wards in Derbyshire' for example. This initial search will enable us to understand which ward our provision sits within and then we will be able to refine our search to access a greater level of information about our community.

What has changed?

There are very few settings that go through a whole year without something of significance happening, but we rarely have the time to analyse the impact of that change or development.

Every time there is a change, this can have both a positive and/or negative impact on what we do, and as someone who will always need to have an accurate view of the quality of our provision, we should be able to understand whether the change has been beneficial, or whether further action is needed.

Consider, for example, the impact of a senior member of staff leaving. When we recruited to fill this vacancy, were we able to find someone who had the same level of expertise and depth of knowledge. If not, have we done everything we can to address this issue?

What about building work – if we have made alterations to our building, there may not be a place in our self-evaluation documents to realise just how much of an impact those alterations made. A bigger room perhaps, or more natural light. Even a larger expanse of wall space can make a difference to the way we use a space and what we can do in it. So, are we recognising and celebrating the positive impact of change?

The views of other professionals

Any external observation of quality is useful because the source will not be immersed in our day-to-day practice, therefore, they may notice things that we haven't seen, and comments are likely to be less subjective. We may not always agree with the findings, but we should seriously consider the points raised and the impact that they may have on practice. These views may come from local authority quality assurance visits, or specialist support services such as a Speech and Language Therapist. We would also include an Ofsted inspection in this category, so let's spend a little more time focusing on the importance of our Ofsted inspection reports.

Inspection actions/recommendations

Ofsted inspections are a regulatory requirement and, therefore, should form part of our self-evaluation picture. Time and time again I read inspection reports which state that the provider has not completed the actions or recommendations from the last inspection to a satisfactory standard (and in some cases the actions have not been carried out at all).

To be clear, Ofsted use the word 'recommendation', which may imply choice - but if the regulatory body has identified a development point, we would be well advised to address it. Addressing an issue a few weeks after our inspection will not be enough if those improvements do not have a long-lasting impact on practice. Inspection reports refer to the need for us to sustain and embed any actions taken which means that inspectors will look to see that practice is now effective at our next inspection point.

This is often a sticking point in inspection reports because of the nature of the inspection cycle. Earlier I shared that each inspection cycle is 4 year long, so if we were inspected at the beginning of one cycle and near the end of another, it could be up to 7 years before we were inspected again. During this period of time Ofsted will expect any actions taken to be embedded in practice, therefore, short bursts of activity after an inspection will have long since passed if we do not ensure that those activities are sustained.

In cases where settings have not sustained or embedded their initial activity, inspectors have no choice other than to record the fact that the issue still remains an area of concern.

This position is likely to cast doubt on the effectiveness of leadership and management. From an inspector's point of view, the setting were asked to make improvements in a particular area, this hasn't been sustains, so one would naturally wonder why the leadership team haven't done more to ensure that this aspect of practice was of a consistently high standard.

It is, therefore, worthwhile dedicating a space toward the top of our self-evaluation documents for regulatory actions and recommendations, because keeping the issue in the forefront of our minds is likely to ensure that the actions taken are sustained over time.

Another reason for placing inspection actions and recommendations toward the top of our self-evaluation document is the distance between inspection visits. If our next inspection point is 7 years later, will we be able to remember what we did, how successful it was and how practice has moved forward between now and then, without some form of documentation to aid our memory?

The bottom line is that a lack of action or sustained activity could result in a lower inspection grade, because we are simply not able to demonstrate effective management within an area which Ofsted felt needed to be improved.

The example over the page uses a fictitious report to highlight how you may want to record this information. You can clearly see the judgements made by an inspector, the steps that we would need to take, and the impact of our actions.

Previous inspection actions/recommendations

No.	Ofsted actions/recommendations	Actions taken to date
1	**Judgement:** There are inconsistencies in the assessments of what children know, understand and can do. This means that some next steps are inappropriate and unlikely to meet the immediate needs of children. **Recommendation:** Ensure that observations and assessments of children's learning are accurate and that they pave the way for appropriate next steps in learning.	Observations and assessments have been thoroughly reviewed throughout the nursery. During this time the management team found that many observations provided a lengthy description of what children were doing, but that assessment information was sparse. This was having a direct impact on staff's understanding of what children know, understand and can do. We have, therefore, spent time training staff to better understand the observation, assessment and planning cycle. We have also reviewed and changed our recording system which now prompts staff to record with a greater level of accuracy. This should lead to secure next steps for learning and development. As part of our monitoring and evaluation activities, senior leaders now sample children's files monthly and compare observations and assessments with direct observations of practice and children at play. Staff strengths and areas for development from both room observations and completed observations/assessments, now feed into performance management discussions.

Impact

Observations and assessments of children now consistently reflect each child's appropriate stage of development, and children's next steps provide an appropriate level of challenge.

The new monthly reviews enable senior leaders to:
- consistently identify gaps in learning,
- ensure breadth and balance of curriculum delivery,
- ensure an appropriate level of challenge for all children,
- moderate judgements, ensuring greater consistency in assessing what children know, understand and can do.

Summarising what you do well and addressing the things that you don't

Just because we use the Ofsted Inspection Handbook to moderate our judgements, does not mean that we have to stick rigidly to the headings used against the grade descriptors. We should work in a way that makes sense to us, whilst ensuring that we cover the breadth of topics that Ofsted will look at, as a minimum. These are the headings that I recommend when supporting early years settings, and the reason why:

Monitoring and evaluating the quality of provision to improve practice and outcomes for children

We have gone to a lot of trouble to create a robust monitoring and evaluation framework, but we need to ensure that it remains fit for purpose and that our monitoring activities continue to provide us with data/information that will help us to understand what is working well and what isn't. We, therefore, need to provide a section in our self-evaluation documents to reflect on the effectiveness of our systems, processes and monitoring activities.

It is here that we would talk about the rigour of our monitoring and evaluation framework and the things we need to change or refine to ensure that we continue to receive accurate and timely data.

Gathering feedback to support improvement planning

Gaining the views of those who work in our setting has been a recurring theme throughout this book. It is a way to ensure that our view of quality remains accurate and that we can test our own perceptions of what is good by gathering a range of evidence which may challenge what we know and understand to be true.

This section should include the personal views and perceptions of members of staff. Ofsted documents regularly talk about what it is like to be a child in our provision, but do we understand what it is like to work in our setting from the perspective of our staff? Some thoughts and feedback may come through performance management activities, but we will need to think more broadly about how we capture and take on board the views of our staff.

What about our relationship with parents or carers? Many settings pride themselves on the relationships they build with parents, but are we doing enough to capture what they think of our setting? We may, therefore, think of organising and including the outcome of surveys, questionnaires and/or personal requests to demonstrate our commitment to partnership working.

Another vitally important part of gathering feedback is how we obtain the voice of our children. What opportunities are there throughout the year to understand how they feel about their environment and the activities and the opportunities we provide for them? Do some comments indicate the need for significant change, which would require further planning?

In all cases, we should document meaningful interactions that have an impact on *what we do* and *how we do* it.

Improving the quality of our safeguarding arrangements to keep children safe

Safeguarding is a huge area of responsibility that seems to get bigger each year, so we need to ensure that we continue to invest time in developing our knowledge, the knowledge of staff and that we continue to review the effectiveness of our safeguarding activities.

These are the types of questions that we may want to answer in our self-evaluation material:

- How do we know that staff understand safeguarding legislation?
- How do we know that staff can successfully implement our safeguarding and child protection policies, particularly with regard to raising concerns about a child, and making allegations against a member of staff or management?
- How can we demonstrate that staff's knowledge and understanding of safeguarding continues to develop, and that they are able to identify behaviours and circumstances that may place children at greater risk of harm; radicalisation and extremism, criminal exploitation such as county-lines, sexual exploitation, domestic violence etc.
- Do we have evidence that the Welfare Requirements continue to be effectively implemented?
- What evidence do we have that our processes to ensure that staff remain suitable to work with children are effective?

Improving the quality of teaching and learning through performance management and professional development

It would be much easier to focus solely on teaching and learning, but in doing so we miss the opportunity to make a direct link between any weaknesses in this area, performance management activities and professional development opportunities. In many of the Ofsted reports that I have read, the management team have been identified as the main reason for poor or inconsistent teaching and learning because staff haven't been supported effectively to address issues in practice. The following extract from my inspection analysis will provide a broader understanding of the issues that Ofsted have identified:

"Management of staff: the supervision of and support given to staff to ensure consistently high-quality provision

- Implement effective supervision arrangements that provide staff with support, coaching and training to raise the quality of teaching and learning.
- Refine staff supervision sessions to effectively identify and address weaknesses in staff practice ensuring that teaching is at a consistently good level.
- Develop staff's on-going opportunities to access professional development and evaluate the impact of those experiences.
- Ensure that staff are clear about their roles, responsibilities and the expectations for practice.
- Ensure that supervision happens regularly and consistently for all members of staff.
- Ensure that effective supervision and monitoring arrangements accurately identify and quickly address weaker areas of practice and teaching."

Source: Inspection Trends: A Report for the Early Years Private, Voluntary & Independent Sector, Early Years Fundamentals, 2018.

It, therefore, makes sense to prompt ourselves to think more widely about issues that concern teaching and learning and what then needs to happen to support individual members of staff, or to address the issues with small groups and/or the whole team.

Our observations of adult: child interactions, the accuracy of observations and assessments, effectiveness of planning, cohort tracking and peer-on-peer assessment will highlight strengths and areas of development that can then be addressed through performance management activities, individually tailored professional development opportunities or whole team training events.

Providing environments that meet the needs and interests of children (including the Characteristics of Effective Learning)

The *quality* of our learning environment can often be overlooked because it's part of teaching and learning, but by separating this area out, we are forcing ourselves to look at it more closely and to think about what we provide and how well it meets the need of our children. This means that there is less likelihood of something important going unnoticed.

Focusing on the quality of the learning environment will enable us to ask ourselves:

- Do we know where children like to play the most, and have we analysed why that is?
- Are there parts of our environment which children do not use often, and do we have thoughts about why this is?
- Have we asked the children to share what they like or don't like about our learning environments both indoors and outdoors?
- Can we see children's interests represented in the environment?
- Do we know why areas have be presented in a particular way? Is there a rationale for this?
- What works well in our environments?
- What changes have we made and what impact are they having? (Do we see a difference in levels of engagement, are children able to be more independent?)

Working in partnership with parents and carers

Parents/carers are a child's primary educator, so we need to continually foster effective working relationships with parents to gain a rounded view of what children know, understand and can do, and to encourage parents to continue to share changes, developments and things that they feel are of importance.

Partnership with parents has been a strength of the early years sector for a number of years and staff work hard to sustain effective relationships because they understand how important it is to have an open, honest and on-going dialogue with parents about the needs of their child. Because of this, much of the good work that happens is overlooked as being a strength and often goes unrecognised in self-evaluation documents. By providing an area that focuses on our relationships with parents and carers, we give staff recognition for their patience, compassion and the support they regular give to children and their families.

is forcing providers to think in more detail about their working relationships with other providers; what we share, how often, and how we work in partnership to complement each other's educational programmes.

Meaningful relationships with parents also mean that we get to know more about what's happening at home. Where there is trust, parents are more likely to share information about things that they are finding difficult which, in turn, puts us in a better place to respond to and meet the needs of each child.

Having a connection with parents also means that we create opportunities to influence learning at home. This is an area, however, that does not feature as a strength in many inspection reports, so it's worth considering what strategies we encourage staff to use. Do we have a whole setting approach to supporting learning at home or are we relying on staff to find opportunities to talk to parents about this? Is our strategy working?

Working with other professionals to provide continuity of care and education

Continuity of care and education is an increasing area of concern in inspection reports. This is more than likely due to the introduction of the additional 15 hours of free nursery education for working parents. Families who meet the income threshold set by the government are now able to access a nursery place for up to 30 hours per week.

However, parents are free to 'spend' their 30 hours in a way which best meets the needs of their family and the demands of work. Consequently, a child could be attending more than 1 setting in any given week, which

Working with external professionals to provide appropriate support and interventions

Relationships with external professionals strengthen what we are able to offer to our children. Practitioners who work alongside specialists such as Speech and Language Therapists, Occupational Therapists or behaviour support services etc., enable staff to improve their knowledge and skills. This, often, has a positive impact on early identification, the quality of our intervention strategies, the environments that we provide and the quality of adult:child interactions.

But do we recognise this joint working as being a strength? And do we reflect on the impact that working with a specialist has had, not only on the progress of children, but on staff? Are there staff members who now have an increased level of knowledge due to their interactions with specialist services?

The headings that have just been discussed are topics that Ofsted will review during an inspection, however, your self-evaluation documents should reflect all of your monitoring activities, including sections for finance, HR, marketing etc.

Recording your findings

Summarising our findings doesn't need to involve writing reams. We need to use short evaluative statements to reflect what we found and what that means. The example below may help you to visualise how all of these elements come together. (A blank version of this self-evaluation template can be found at Annex G).

Even though we have developed a robust monitoring framework based on legislative requirements, we will still need to refer to the Ofsted Early Years Inspection Handbook.

We may feel that what we do is a strength, but the grade descriptors in the Inspection Handbook will provide additional confirmation.

Monitoring and evaluating the quality of provision to improve practice and outcomes for children

Key strengths:	How we know that these areas are strengths:	
Although parts of our monitoring and evaluation system have recently been reviewed, we have an embedded 12-month cycle of monitoring activities in place. Activities focus on the quality of teaching and learning, the progress of children, performance management, the environment, safeguarding, early intervention, policies into practice and the welfare requirements. All staff are aware of the monitoring timetable and the different roles assigned to individual team members. The senior leadership team has invested time in setting clear expectations for practice which are reviewed as part of our monitoring activities. Monitoring activities are shared across the team, which includes the Manager, the Deputy, the SENDCo, the Safeguarding Lead and Room Leaders. Peer-on-peer reviews also form part of our monitoring activities.	Our approach is methodical and systematic, which provides a clear view of our strengths and areas for development. We include all of our team in monitoring activities which gives a far more rounded view of what we know and understand about the quality of our provision. From the information gained from our monitoring activities, we are able to identify appropriate priorities for improvement and put action plans in place to address any issues we find. Areas for development and/or priorities for improvement also feed directly into our performance management activities. Staff have development targets that focus on professional development and setting priorities. This approach ensures continual improvement.	
Areas for development:	**Plans/priorities for the future:**	**By when:**
Because we have recently extended our opening hours, we now need to create a group in the tracker for children attending for more than 28 hours a week. The key question we need to answer is: do children make more progress if they stay longer?	Adapt the tracker to include a '30 hours' group.	03/06/2019
Work that has taken place:	**The impact/difference our actions made**	
We have reviewed our monitoring activities for observations and assessment. The senior leadership team now sample and moderate children's files on a monthly basis and confirm the accuracy of judgements by comparing written reports with direct observations of children at play.	The new monthly reviews are enabling senior leaders to identify gaps in learning more readily and ensure greater consistency in assessing what children know, understand and can do.	

Source: Early Years Fundamentals Ltd. Early Years Self Evaluation Framework, 2018.

Ensuring the inspector sees your self-evaluation materials before the inspection

Historically anyone who used the Ofsted SEF would have been able to upload the completed or updated document to the Ofsted online portal, but the withdrawal of the SEF means that this facility is no longer available. However, there are two things that we can do to increase the likelihood of the inspector reading our self-evaluation documents prior to an inspection:

1. Use your website

If we have a dedicated website, it may be worth uploading any useful or relevant self-evaluation documents here. Inspectors are obliged to look at the setting's website, before they carry out an inspection.

2. Email it direct

When the inspector initially makes contact, the day before our inspection, we could take the opportunity to send by email all our self-evaluation documentation to him/her at this time.

By doing either of those actions, we are providing the inspector with the opportunity to get to know our setting a bit better before they visit.

Action planning

Action plans help us to address weaker areas of practice. They provide a structure that enables us to capture where we are now, where we need to be and how we intend to get there. They are the documents that always sit at the front of my self-evaluation folder because they reflect the work that I am involved in now, and because I am likely to add notes to them frequently, as I record when individual actions have been completed, when things don't go according to plan and when I have evidence of impact.

There is no standardised format for an action plan, but most templates contain the following:

- an issue to be solved or a piece of work that needs to be taken forward,
- the actions to be taken,
- success criteria,
- the name of the person responsible for the action,
- when it should be completed by,
- some way of recording that actions have/ have not been taken,
- the impact or difference that all or any of those actions have made.

Action plans should be open, transparent and shared with staff (unless they contain sensitive information about changes to staffing or things that will affect staff). They should also be updated at several points in the year to reflect the setting's progress so far.

Including staff in this process creates a deeper level of trust and understanding, (as has been previously established) but it is also a powerful motivator. If a staff member has been assigned an action and they know that the plan will regularly be updated, actions are far more likely to be completed by the date set!

Action plans are also a useful source of information when it comes to performance management discussions. They can help us to reflect on the achievements of staff or help to identify areas of concern.

An example of a more detailed action plan, which also identifies and tracks changes and challenges along the way, is opposite. If you find this useful, there is a blank template at Annex H.

Action planning template

Origin of the issue: Moderation of staff's observations, assessment and next steps

| **Action plan for:** The Characteristics of Effective Learning (COEL) | **Person responsible:** Ann | | Date range: Feb – July 2019 | |

Issue:	**Actions needed:**	**Who:**	**By when:**
Staff do not consistently report on the COEL in their observations of children, therefore we do not have a holistic view of the child as a learner.	Hold a staff training session on understanding and implementing the COEL.	Ann	05/06/2019
	Review the format of observation templates with staff to ensure that the COEL are recorded consistently.	Ann & staff team	05/06/2019
	Set expectations for observations and assessment using WAGOLL (what a good one looks like).	Ann & Bea	14/06/2019
	Hold a staff meeting to talk through expectations and WAGOLL examples.	Ann	05/06/2019

What difference do we hope this will make?	**How will actions be monitored?**	**When:**	**Date this happened**
Staff will have a better understanding of the importance of the COEL. Staff will be able to use the input from the training session to develop their approach to recording and reporting against the COEL. This will provide a more rounded view of each child as a learner, enabling us to better meet the individual needs of our children.	Manager will attend the staff meeting on the COEL and review the progress made.	05/06/2019	05/06/2019
	The EY consultant from the LA will review progress against this action plan during our annual review.	20/06/2019	20/06/2019
	Manager will support the Deputy to set expectations for observations during a staff meeting.	05/03/2019	Delayed until 28/05/2019
	Manager will review the use of the new format through the monthly sampling of children's files.	Monthly	04/06/2019 01/07/2019

What impact/difference have our actions made?	**If actions were not completed, state the reason here**
Staff are now clear about the expectations for recording and reporting on the COEL. In the first sample of staff observations, there was a marked improvement in the information provided.	The staff meeting held on the COEL clearly identified that some staff members lack confidence in the area of creating and thinking critically, therefore the April staff meeting will focus on how we support children to plan, make decisions and to become problem solvers.

Is there anything else that we need to do, or are the actions complete?	**List any actions that need to be followed up in a new action plan**
JH was unable to attend the staff meeting on COEL, therefore time will need to be spent with JH to ensure that she has accessed the key messages from the session.	N/A

Source: Early Years Fundamentals Ltd. Early Years Self Evaluation Framework, 2018.

This is far more detailed than the action plans used by most settings. The main reason for this is that I would use this document regularly to track progress, and to identify and address challenges. This particular format highlights impact, monitors progress and provides the ability for us to make changes to plans where things are not going as anticipated. On the next pages are detailed reasons why the headings in the example above have been used.

Reasons for the key headings of the action plan

Key heading	Reason
Origin	Where the issue or piece of work came from is important as it will influence the order in which we address our priorities and how quickly something needs to be done. For example, a recommendation from Ofsted is likely to be of greater importance than an action to develop a newsletter for parents.
Date range	An action plan should take place within a defined period of time. If actions are not completed within this timeframe it may indicate bigger problems or that we have underestimated the complexity of the work required.
Area of practice	It is helpful for everyone concerned to understand the focus of the action plan.
Person responsible	In larger settings or where there are several members of the senior leadership team, it is useful to identify someone that will take overall responsibility for moving the plan forward and for monitoring that actions have been taken.
The issue or concern	We need to clearly identify the problem, issue or piece of work that needs to be addressed/undertaken.
The actions	The issue needs to be broken down into steps that will enable us to thoroughly address it.
Who will take responsibility for each action	We will need to assign someone to take responsibility for each action to ensure that there are clear lines of accountability.
When it will be completed	Without a deadline for completion, there is no sense of urgency, and actions could remain unresolved. Uncompleted actions may stop others from getting on with the tasks that they have been assigned.

Reasons for the key headings of the action plan

Key heading	Reason
The difference we hope the action will make	We need to have a clear vision of where we want to be. By identifying what that will look like, staff members have a clear understanding of what is expected and how their actions contribute to the bigger picture.
How the action will be monitored	This is a step that is often overlooked because it is seen as unimportant. It is actually crucial to the success of the action plan, as without monitoring activities no-one is checking to make sure whether actions have been taken and if they remain fit for purpose.
When we expect the monitoring activity to happen	
A date column to record when monitoring activities happened	Not essential, but it is another measure to ensure that our own monitoring activities (or those of others) don't slip off the radar.
The impact or difference our actions have made	One of THE most important boxes to complete. There is no point taking action if we do not then take the time to understand whether they have made a difference or whether we need to rethink our plans.
When actions didn't happen and why. (Appears on the template as 'If actions were not completed, state the reason here')	In the natural cycle of an action plan, there are likely to be things that do not go according to plan, but they should not be ignored. By identifying any barrier or challenge we can reshape our plan to ensure that we thoroughly and systematically address the issue.
Actions that have occurred to us as we progress through the plan. (Appears on the template as 'Is there anything else that we need to do, or are the actions complete?')	When action plans become a working document, it is likely that other tasks may occur to us as we go along. If we store our plans electronically it is easy to add them to our action column, but many settings still use paper copies because it is an easier way to share information. If you are a setting that uses paper copies you may find it easier to have a column to record additional actions instead of having to amend and then reprint and distribute new copies.
Any actions that need to be followed up in a new action plan	As we get towards the end of an action planning cycle, there may be things that haven't been completed. It is worth making a note of these issues so that they can be taken forward into the next set of action plans. Focusing on one small box is far easier than having to wade through the whole plan looking for things that need to be carried forward.

Setting actions or targets

The success of any action plan is dependent on the way we write our actions. The same can be said for the way in which we construct performance management targets, so rather than duplicate the same table twice, (in both the performance management chapter and this one) I have created one table that deals with setting actions and targets for performance management together.

Whether we are designing an action plan to address priorities for improvement or documenting performance management targets in our 1:1 discussions with staff, it is useful to use the well-known acronym S.M.A.R.T.E.R targets to help us produce clear and concise plans that can be understood by everyone.

The table below applies the S.M.A.R.T.E.R acronym to both of these areas.

Writing an action plan or performance management targets

Developing an action plan for improvement	Developing performance targets
Specific – Each action/target needs to clearly communicate/describe what action needs to be taken.	
Measurable – We need to describe how we will know when each action/target has been achieved. This is also an opportunity to be clear about our expectations; a target/action can be completed, but not necessarily meet the standards that we have set for practice. For example, the creative area was rearranged with the intention of children being able to access resources independently, however, the staff member has restricted the amount of resources that are available because s/he doesn't want children 'to make a mess'. Technically, the task was fulfilled as children can now access resources independently, but the choice is so limited that learning opportunities have been significantly reduced.	
Agreed – We need to make sure that we have communicated the actions we have assigned to those concerned. Everyone involved needs time to read and understand the plan and then come back to us with any queries or concerns about their actions.	**Agreed** – Although the member of staff may verbally agree to targets that we assign during our 1:1 meeting, this could be retracted at a later stage or easily misunderstood. It is, therefore, suggested that performance management records are signed by the manager and the staff member to show that the document is an accurate reflection of their conversation. (This needs to be done as close to the event as possible, whilst memories are still fresh!)
Realistic – We need to consider what each action entails and how quickly it needs to be completed. Is this doable? Is it likely to add greatly to the workload of the staff member? We also need to consider whether the staff member has the skills and/or knowledge to do what is being asked of them; might training or mentoring be required first? What about the actual actions? Have we created manageable steps? Smaller steps initially may help to build confidence and to ensure that the action/target is completed without struggling.	
Timebound – There needs to be a date set for completion, otherwise actions will drag on or not be undertaken. Without a deadline for completion, there is no incentive to get things done.	
Evaluated – We need space to reflect on what has been achieved so far and how successful the actions taken have been. Did we achieve what we set out to do? If not, why not? What was the impact? What difference has the action made to our children, environments, staff, systems/processes or parents?	
Recorded – Regularly updating our action plans will enable us to quickly see which actions are still pending and which have been completed.	**Recorded** – Keeping a record of our conversations with staff enables us to track the journey that has been taken so far and to establish whether things are improving…or not!

There is no requirement for you to use the earlier example provided, and you may prefer to use something with fewer boxes…or you may want to consider using Excel.

Those of us who have worked in early years for quite some time will appreciate that most of the templates we use in our settings consist of A4 sheets of paper that we can blow up or reduce on a photocopier. However, with regular access to PCs and a growing reliance on IT, there might be a more efficient and quicker way of producing an action plan.

Action logs (just another name for an action plan) are used widely in industry to keep track of actions set within teams. They contain the same information as an action plan, but are produced in Excel (on a spreadsheet). Using this format means that we are no longer constrained by having to keep things handwritten in neat little boxes and the data can be presented in columns next to each other.

The beauty of writing an action plan in Excel is that we can sort our data using filters which will completely revolutionise any standard action planning process. We can sort by actions, deadline, name, or filter by origin or area. We use exactly the same headings, but enter the data in columns, making it easier to search and follow information across a page.

Imagine being able to filter by 'deadline' to see if all our actions have been completed for this month, or filtering

by the name of a staff member so that we can give them a personalised list of actions. What about searching by 'area' to review all the work that has taken place in teaching and learning over the last 12 months? It has phenomenal capacity and could make life far easier.

Don't forget Trello! If you prefer to use cloud-based technology and/or something that is more visually appealing than an Excel spreadsheet, Trello may just be the tool you've been looking for. (See Chapter 2)

Origin	Area	Person Responsible	Issue	Action	Responsible for the Action	Complete By

Final thoughts

Effective monitoring and evaluation systems take time to build and require a great deal of self-reflection, honest conversations about what we know and don't know, and what is working well and what isn't, but they are always easier to construct when we involve others in their design.

The processes and frameworks outlined in this book will help you to rigorously interrogate practice, to better understand your organisation, to manage risk and to ensure that your improvement activities are focused on the things that will make the biggest difference to children, parents, staff and the profitability of your business.

Wherever possible, I have given explanations of why things are important to provide a sound basis for activity, there are two main reasons for this:

1. Understanding the reason or theory behind any area of practice enables us to extract the key messages and then to put it into practice in a way that is both meaningful and manageable. It also gives us the confidence to be able to adapt our approach when needed.

2. Every change to the Ofsted inspection framework raises the quality bar, therefore, we need methodical and systematic ways to ensure that we continue to meet the standards set. Although monitoring and evaluation isn't something we do to satisfy Ofsted, the thoroughness and effectiveness of our systems will continue to be tested at the point of inspection.

   Ofsted inspection outcomes are directly linked to a provider's local authority funding, therefore, anything less than a 'good' could result in a loss of revenue. It is, therefore, of paramount importance that we can articulate what we do, how effective this is and the difference our provision makes to the lives of the children who attend the setting.

Lastly, ensure that you take every opportunity to identify and celebrate all the phenomenal things that you do for your children and their families.

Annex A – Forming your WHY, HOW, WHAT

Why (Our purpose):

No. (e.g.1)	How are we going to make it happen?	No. (e.g. 1.1)	What will we see if we've been successful? (Outcomes for success)	Actions that need to be taken

Annex B – Mapping actions against levels of responsibility

Levels of responsibility →

Actions ↓	√	Notes	√	Notes	√	Notes

Annex C - Mapping inspections actions and recommendations against the National Professional Qualification Content and Assessment Framework

Inspection Actions and Recommendations from Requires Improvement and Inadequate Inspection Reports

Monitoring & Self-Evaluation
- Monitor and evaluate the impact of teaching and practice, identify inconsistencies and provide staff with professional development opportunities to help raise the quality of teaching to a consistently good level.
- Ensure that children's needs are met effectively through accurate assessment and planning.
- Improve staff's skills and knowledge further across all areas of learning to ensure that children receive a broad and balanced curriculum. (Many recommendations on the development of communication skills and the extension of vocabulary.)
- Develop effective systems for self-evaluation, identifying strengths and weaknesses, and putting plans in place to swiftly and continually improve provision.
- Enhance arrangement to monitor the quality of the provision to ensure that all policies and procedures are consistently implemented.
- Further develop the self-evaluation process to include the views of children and parents.
- Improve procedures to ensure that the impact of additional funding is monitored. (Early Years Pupil Premium)
- Use self-evaluation effectively to identify any breaches of the welfare requirements.

Monitoring Progress & Outcomes
- Develop systems to effectively monitor and track the progress of individuals and groups.
- Monitor the progress of groups so that teaching can be more effectively targeted to gaps in learning.
- Monitor educational programmes to ensure that all children have access to a broad and balanced curriculum.
- Use monitoring and tracking systems consistently to ensure that all children are making good progress.

National Professional Qualification Content and Assessment Framework teaches participants how to:

Design a sustainable business development strategy, whether for growth, stabilisation or specialisation (pg.30)

Identify and anticipate changes in the external or strategic environment and understand their impact on different organisations (pg.30)

Analyse performance data to identify the causes of variation within a school and against comparative schools (for example, in relation to national benchmarks, historical performance or between different groups) (pg.17)

Ensure data collected is necessary, proportionate and manageable for staff (pg.17)

Work with the governing board effectively to identify and agree approaches to school priorities (pg.17)

Design and implement sustainable change across a school (pg.17)

Identify a range of local and national partners that can support school improvement (pg.19)

Annex C - Mapping inspections actions and recommendations against the National Professional Qualification Content and Assessment Framework *Continued*

Inspection Actions and Recommendations from Requires Improvement and Inadequate Inspection Reports

Observation, Assessment & Next Steps

- Ensure that all staff complete regular and accurate assessments that provide a clear view of what children know, understand and can do.
- Use assessment information consistently to plan appropriate next steps in development and learning.
- Use information from parents to help establish starting points on entry.
- Ensure that observation and assessments focus on children's interests as well as next steps.
- Ensure that observations and assessments are provided for all areas of learning giving a rounded view of what children know, understand and can do.

Planning & Challenge

- Use information from on-going observations and assessments to plan appropriate challenges for all children.
- Plan challenging and enjoyable experiences for children that take into account their individual needs, interests and abilities, including children who need extra support.
- Ensure activities are appropriately differentiated, taking account of children's ages, interests, and levels of understanding.
- Ensure adults plan meaningful activities, which cover all areas of learning. (Many recommendations requested more focus on similarities and differences, the use of number and problem-solving skills, early writing opportunities and physical development).
- Ensure staff assess children's skills and use this information to plan an exciting mix of adult-led and child-initiated activities that challenge children and meet their needs.

The Learning Environment

- Ensure the learning environment both in and outdoors provides well-resourced and well-planned activities that meet the needs and interest of all children.
- Ensure the organisation of the environment supports children to become more independent, enabling them to follow their ideas and interests throughout the session/day.
- Structure the environment to reduce disruptions and distractions whilst children learn.
- Ensure equipment is well maintained, safe and suitable especially where children of varying ages access the same space.
- Make better use of indoors and outdoors to provide more stimulating environments which keep children engaged and motivated to learn.

Managing Behaviour

- Provide children with clear messages about what is expected of them through the day.
- Ensure staff understand the setting's behaviour management policy and that this is implemented consistently.
- Ensure staff have the appropriate skills and knowledge to support children to form positive relationships and to learn how to manage their own feelings and behaviour.
- Develop and deploy effective strategies to support children who display challenging behaviour.
- Ensure written records are kept when physical intervention has been used and that parents are informed the same day.

Key Person

- Provide a key person for each child, ensuring that parents know who their child's key person is.
- Ensure that the key person system effectively meets the individual needs of each child.
- Ensure that key person arrangements provide effective two-way communications with parents.

Supporting children with English as an Additional Language (EAL)

- Ensure that children whose home language is not English have opportunities to use, hear and play in their home language.
- Plan and target opportunities to practice and develop spoken language in readiness for moving to school.
- Provide appropriately challenging learning experiences for children whose home language is not English.

National Professional Qualification Content and Assessment Framework teaches participants how to:

Use a range of techniques to gather evidence on teaching quality and the impact of interventions across a school (pg.18)

Assess and improve teaching quality, pupil progress and attainment in a range of different contexts, including for disadvantaged pupils or those with particular needs, for example, including Pupil Premium, SEND, EAL or the most able pupils (pg.31)

Develop and maintain a rich, high-quality school curriculum (pg.18)

Annex C - Mapping inspections actions and recommendations against the National Professional Qualification Content and Assessment Framework *Continued*

Inspection Actions and Recommendations from Requires Improvement and Inadequate Inspection Reports
Management of Staff ■ Ensure that staff develop a robust understanding of assessment systems that enable them to monitor progress and identify gaps in learning. ■ Robustly review the progress of children to ensure that assessments are accurate and any gaps in learning are addressed swiftly. ■ Make better use of information gained from assessments to understand the progress that children are making and where teaching needs to be targeted.
National Professional Qualification Content and Assessment Framework teaches participants how to:
Hold all staff to account for performance using performance management, appraisal, misconduct and grievance systems (pg.29) Create and sustain an environment where all staff are encouraged to develop their own knowledge and skills, and support each other Anticipate capability requirements or gaps in the school and design strategies to fill them (pg.29) Identify excellent professional development practice Identify talent within an organisation and put in place arrangements or tools to develop and retain it Design professional development strategies, which engage all staff (including new/recently qualified teachers) and anticipate future professional development needs (Pg.22)

Inspection Actions and Recommendations from Requires Improvement and Inadequate Inspection Reports
Partnership with Parents ■ Ensure that detailed information is gathered from parents about what their child knows and can do when they first start nursery to support planning. ■ Engage with parents to encourage them to contribute more information about their child's learning. ■ Improve communication with parents to ensure that their views are given due consideration when planning for improvements. ■ Make the most of opportunities to keep parents informed about their child's progress. **Working in partnership with other professionals** ■ Develop systems for sharing information with other providers to offer a more consistent learning experience. ■ Strengthen partnership working with other providers, sharing information to support complimentary learning experiences. ■ Obtain more information about what children are learning from other settings.
National Professional Qualification Content and Assessment Framework teaches participants how to:
Identify the most effective partnerships for improving pupil progress (Pg.20)

Source: Early Years Fundamentals Ltd, 2018. Source: DfE, 2017.

Annex D – Risk Mapping

Actions	Low	Medium		High		What is my rationale for the level of risk?
	1	2	3	4	5	

Annex E – How to create a rigorous and manageable monitoring framework

Actions	What type of monitoring needs to take place?		Expectations for practice/criteria/standard
	A quick check that this has been done	In-depth (What needs to be monitored)	How we will judge the effectiveness of practice (What will we look for or at)

Annex F – Performance review template

Name of Employee:		Name of Manager:	
Date of meeting:		Date of next meeting:	

Targets set in last review

Target:	Complete by:		
	Achieved on:		
Progress to date:			Challenges or barriers to success:

Target:	Complete by:		
	Achieved on:		
Progress to date:			Challenges or barriers to success:

Target:	Complete by:		
	Achieved on:		
Progress to date:			Challenges or barriers to success:

Annex F – Performance review template *Continued*

Training & development opportunities

Date:	Course/opportunity	Level:	Duration:

What difference has this made to your practice?

Main points of our discussion

Discussion:	Targets & actions for this meeting:	Who for?	Complete by:

Training & development opportunities

Date:	Course/opportunity	Level:	Duration:

Expected outcome

Date:	Course/opportunity	Level:	Duration:

Expected outcome

Signed as an accurate record

Name of Employee:	Name of Manager:
Date:	Date:

Source: EYF Performance management templates 2018

Annex G – A self-evaluation template

Key strengths:	How we know that these areas are strengths:	

Areas for development:	Plans/priorities for the future:	When:

Work that has taken place:	Impact/difference our actions have made	

Source: Early Years Fundamentals Ltd. Early Years Self Evaluation Framework, 2018.

Annex H – An action planning template

Origin of the issue:				
Action plan for:				
Person responsible:		**Date range:**		

Issue:	Actions needed:	Who:	By when:

What difference do we expect this to make?	How will actions be monitored?	When:	Date this happened

What impact/difference have our actions made?	If actions were not completed, state the reason here

Is there anything else that we need to do, or are the actions complete?	List any actions that need to be followed up in a new action plan

Source: Early Years Fundamentals Ltd. Early Years Self Evaluation Framework, 2018.

References

- Berkeley Human Resources (2018) **Performance** [Online]. Berkeley University. [Accessed 8 July 2018]. Available from: https://hr.berkeley.edu/performance/performance-management

- CIPD (2018) **Performance management: an introduction** [Online]. CIPD [Accessed 8 July 2018]. Available from: https://www.cipd.co.uk/knowledge/fundamentals/people/performance/factsheet

- Cope, A. (2018) **Leadership: The multiplier effect**. London: Hodder & Stoughton.

- Department for Education (DfE). (2018a). **Early education and childcare Statutory guidance for local authorities**. [Online]. DfE: Crown. [Accessed 4 July 2018]. Available from: https://assets.publishing.service.gov.uk/government/uploads/system/uploads/attachment_data/file/718179/Early_education_and_childcare-statutory_guidance.pdf

- Department for Education (DfE). (2017a) **National Professional Qualification for Headship (NPQH)** [Online]. DfE: Crown. [Accessed 15 November 2018]. Available from: https://www.gov.uk/guidance/national-professional-qualification-for-headship-npqh

- Department for Education (DfE). (2014) **National Professional Qualification in Integrated Centre Leadership (NPQICL)** [Online]. DfE: Crown. [Accessed 12 November 2018]. Available from: https://www.nationalcollege.org.uk/?q=node/644

- Department for Education (DfE). (2017b) **National Professional Qualification (NPQ) Content and Assessment Framework A guide for NPQ participants** [Online]. DfE: Crown. [Accessed 15 November 2018]. Available from: https://assets.publishing.service.gov.uk/government/uploads/system/uploads/attachment_data/file/653046/NPQ_Content_and_Assessment_Framework.pdf

- Early Years Fundamentals Ltd. (EYF). (2018) **Inspection Trends: A Report for the Early Years Private, Voluntary & Independent Sector** [Online]. EYF. [Accessed 3 December 2018]. Available from: https://www.eyfundamentals.org/publications

- Early Years Fundamentals Ltd. (EYF). (2018) **Performance Management Templates** [Online]. EYF. [Accessed 8 December 2018]. Available from: https://www.eyfundamentals.org/publications

- Harris, A. & Lambert, L. (2003) **Building Leadership Capacity for School Improvement**. Maidenhead. Open University Press.

- Harris, A. (2014) **Distributed leadership**. [Online]. Australian Council for Educational Research. [Accessed on 14 December 2018]. Available from: https://www.teachermagazine.com.au/articles/distributed-leadership

- Jones, M., & Harris, A. (2013) **Disciplined Collaboration: Professional Learning with Impact**. Professional Development Today, 15(4), pp. 13-23

- Mind Tools (2018) **Performance Appraisals: Getting Real Results From Performance Reviews** [Online]. Mind Tools. {Accessed 28 September 2018}. Available from: https://www.mindtools.com/community/pages/article/newTMM_32.php?route=pages/article/newTMM_32.php&route=pages/article/newTMM_32.php&

- Mind Tools (2018) **Risk Analysis and Risk Management: Evaluating and Managing Risks** [Online]. Mind Tools. [Accessed 18 October 2018]. Available from: https://www.mindtools.com/pages/article/newTMC_07.htm

- Mullins, L, J. (2016) Management and Organisational Behaviour 11th edn Essex: Prentice Hall.

- Office for Standards in Education, Children's Services and Skills (Ofsted). (2018c). **The Early Years Inspection Handbook**. [Online]. Ofsted: Crown. [Accessed 8 July 2018]. Available from: https://www.gov.uk/government/publications/inspecting-registered-early-years-providers-guidance-for-inspectors

- Oxford Living Dictionary (2018) 'Delegate' [Online]. Oxford University Press. [Accessed 18 December 2018]. Available from: https://en.oxforddictionaries.com/definition/delegate

- Oxford Living Dictionary (2018) 'Appraisal' [Online]. Oxford University Press. [Accessed 18 December 2018]. Available from: https://en.oxforddictionaries.com/definition/appraisal

- Satell, G. (2015) **How to define your organisations values** [Online]. Forbes. [Accessed 26 November 2018]. Available from: https://www.forbes.com/sites/gregsatell/2015/11/27/how-to-define-your-organizations-values/#3e55605e4054

- Sinek, S. (2009) **Start with why**. New York: Portfolio Penguin.

- The Cambridge English Dictionary (2018) 'Appraisal' [Online]. Cambridge University Press. [Accessed 18 December 2018]. Available from: https://dictionary.cambridge.org/dictionary/english/appraisal

- The International Bureau of Education (2017) **Education: Concept of Governance** [Online]. UNESCO. [Accessed 10 October 2018]. Available from: http://www.ibe.unesco.org/en/geqaf/technical-notes/concept-governance

- Trello (2015) **Getting started video**. [Online]. Atlassian. [Accessed 2 January 2019]. Available from: https://help.trello.com/article/899-getting-started-video-demo

Acknowledgements

Writing an assignment, dissertation, an article for a magazine or even issuing advice in a newsletter can be hard, as I'm sure many of you will agree, so I am extremely lucky to have my amazingly supportive family around me who have always had words of encouragement while I was writing this book. I am particularly indebted to my husband Mark, who has helped me reframe my thinking when I couldn't find the right words. Despite the demands of his own job, he has always made time to read the multiples of drafts and amendments I've made.

I would also like to thank my two girls, Abi and Izzy. Due to their support the washing still got done, the hoovering and cleaning happened regularly and every so often cups of tea or coffee would appear at exactly the right moment. This has been incredibly important because at the time of writing, my company Early Years Fundamentals is still a young company which takes up a great deal of time. Writing this book has meant some very early starts and late nights, and during that time they have shown me nothing but patience, understanding and kindness.

Lastly, I would like to thank Practical Pre-School Books for giving me the opportunity and platform to share my views, thoughts and research with the wider world.